Ordnance Survey

SCOTTISH BORDERS

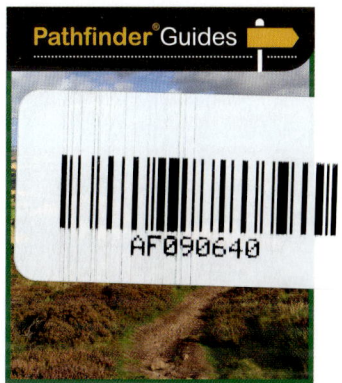

Outstanding Circular Walks

Compiled by Felicity Martin

Contents			
At-a-glance	2	Short walks up to 2½ hours	9
Keymap	4	Slightly harder walks of 2½–4 hours	35
Introduction	5	Longer walks of 4½ hours and over	64
		Further Information	92

At-a-glance

	Walk	Page	🖊	🏠	🚩	⛰	⏱
1	River Teviot and Wilton Lodge Park	10	Common Haugh car park, Hawick	NT 500146	2¼ miles (3.7km)	80ft (25m)	1 hr
2	Gordon Community Woodland	12	Gordon Community Woodland	NT 661436	2¼ miles (3.5km)	35ft (10m)	1 hr
3	Lees Haugh and Leet Water	14	Home Park, Coldstream	NT 840396	3¼ miles (5.2km)	50ft (15m)	1½ hrs
4	Caerlee and the River Tweed	16	Hall Street, Innerleithen	NT 328367	3½ miles (5.8km)	360ft (110m)	1¾ hrs
5	Ven Law and Soonhope	18	Edinburgh Road, Peebles	NT 254405	3¾ miles (6km)	540ft (165m)	2 hrs
6	Ettrick Water Circuit, Selkirk	20	Victoria Park car park, Selkirk	NT 464288	4¼ miles (7km)	55ft (15m)	2 hrs
7	Hen Poo and Duns Castle	22	Market Square, Duns	NT 785538	4¼ miles (6.8km)	375ft (115m)	2 hrs
8	Peniel Heugh	24	Harestanes Visitor Centre	NT 641244	4½ miles (7.4km)	625ft (190m)	2¼ hrs
9	Eyemouth Fort and Pocklaw Slap	26	Harbour Road, Eyemouth	NT 946643	4½ miles (7.2km)	330ft (100m)	2¼ hrs
10	Cockburnspath and Cove	29	The Square, Cockburnspath	NT 774711	5 miles (8km)	510ft (155m)	2½ hrs
11	St Boswells, Dryburgh and the River Tweed	32	St Boswells	NT 593309	5 miles (7.9km)	440ft (135m)	2½ hrs
12	Whiteadder Valley and Edin's Hall Broch	36	Abbey St Bathans	NT 762618	5¼ miles (8.5km)	755ft (230m)	2¾ hrs
13	Arnton Fell	38	Arnton fell	NT 514932	5¼ miles (8.4km)	1,115ft (340m)	3 hrs
14	Melrose and the Eildon Hills	40	Market cross, Melrose	NT 547339	5¼ miles (8.4km)	1,475ft (450m)	3 hrs
15	Buckholm Circular, Galashiels	43	Halliburton, Galashiels	NT 489367	5½ miles (8.7km)	740ft (225m)	3 hrs
16	Coldingham Bay and St Abb's Head	46	Coldingham Bay	NT 915665	5¾ miles (9.1km)	935ft (285m)	3 hrs
17	Selkirk Hill, Whitmuirhill Loch and Lindean Loch	48	Selkirk Hill car park	NT 483 281	5¾ miles (9.25km)	710ft (215m)	3 hrs
18	Peebles and the River Tweed	51	Swimming Pool car park, Peebles	NT 249403	7¼ miles (11.8km)	490ft (150m)	3½ hrs
19	Kelso, Roxburgh and the River Teviot	54	Town Hall, Kelso	NT 727339	7½ miles (12.1km)	360ft (110m)	3½ hrs
20	Denholm Dean and Bedrule	57	Denholm Green	NT 568184	7¼ miles (11.6km)	1,050ft (320m)	3¾ hrs
21	Lauder Common Circular	61	Lauder	NT 530472	7¾ miles (12.5km)	900ft (275m)	4 hrs
22	Dere Street and Mount Ulston	65	Canongate car park, Jedburgh	NT 651205	8½ miles (13.75km)	900ft (275m)	4½ hrs
23	Cauldshiels Loch and the River Tweed	68	Gun Knowe Loch, Tweedbank	NT 517346	10 miles (16.3km)	1,180ft (360m)	5 hrs
24	Kirk Yetholm and the Halterburn Valley	71	Kirk Yetholm	NT 827281	8½ miles (13.7km)	1,985ft (605m)	4¾ hrs
25	St Mary's Loch Circuit	74	South end of St Mary's Loch	NT 238204	9½ miles (15.3km)	655ft (200m)	4¾ hrs
26	Traquair and Minch Moor	79	South of Innerleithen	NT 335357	10 miles (16km)	1,505ft (460m)	5¼ hrs
27	Yarrowford, Minchmoor Road and Three Brethren	83	Lay-by on A708, Yarrowford	NT 408299	9½ miles (15.1km)	1,785ft (545m)	5½ hrs
28	Southern Upland Way and Leaderfoot	87	Abbey car park, Melrose	NT 547341	10¼ miles (16.4km)	1,280ft (390m)	5½ hrs

Comments

Tarmac paths lead through an attractive park on the banks of the River Teviot, passing Hawick Museum in Wilton Lodge as well as statues, an ornamental fountain and a Victorian-style bandstand.

The villagers of Gordon bought 200 acres of woodland in 2001 and turned it into a delightful place for peaceful recreation, with a network of paths, picnic benches, willow sculptures and a pond.

Lees Haugh is a flat and fertile plain inside a large loop of the River Tweed, which here marks the border between Scotland and England. It is separated from Coldstream by tree-lined Leet Water.

The outward part of this walk follows a cycle path beside the River Tweed. It then climbs steadily through woods to Caerlee. The panorama is delightful from the earthworks of the hilltop Iron Age settlement.

This circuit of Soonhope Glen has lovely views over fields and up to the wooded heights of Glentress Forest. It is overlooked by Ven Law, which has traces of numerous prehistoric settlements.

Starting in the middle of Selkirk, this walk in two parts follows Ettrick Water south then takes a loop north along its banks. At Philiphaugh it passes an old mill, salmon viewing centre, café and battlefield.

From a prehistoric fort on Duns Law, the view extends over the handsome small town of Duns to the distant Cheviots. This walk circuits Duns Castle Estate, via a wildlife-rich lake, woods and parkland.

The Waterloo Monument rising above the wooded flanks of Peniel Heugh is a prominent landmark and great viewpoint, and is visited from the craft and visitor centre at Harestanes.

Eyemouth is the major fishing harbour of the Scottish Borders and the site of a 16th-century fort and Gunsgreen House. The Berwickshire Coastal Path leads along rugged clifftops with wonderful views.

This walk starts along the John Muir Way and finishes on the Southern Upland Way, which ends at Cockburnspath. It visits Dunglass Collegiate Church and passes the clifftop fishing village of Cove.

From pretty St Boswells, St Cuthbert's Way leads along the south bank of the River Tweed. On the north bank the Borders Abbeys Way passes Dryburgh Abbey and a landscape designed 200 years ago.

Set above the unspoiled valley of Whiteadder Water, Edin's Hall Broch is one of the finest examples of surviving Iron Age architecture in the region.

Overlooking Hermitage Castle on the edge of the 'Disputed Lands', Arnton Fell offers an enjoyable hill walk and stunning views in an area often ignored by ramblers.

The distinctive profile of the Eildon Hills is glimpsed from several of the walks in this collection. They are ascended here from the old town of Melrose, famous for its abbey and walled flower garden.

Buckholm Hill rises on the north side of bustling Galashiels, which lies below a path that contours the hill's southern slopes. This circuit passes haunted Buckholm Tower and tragic Dobes Grave.

The cliff scenery at St Abb's Head is among the most dramatic on the east coast and it is explored in this walk beginning from the superb sandy cove of Coldingham Bay.

Selkirk Hill gives a bird's-eye view over the town. From there the walk runs over undulating high ground, passing the oldest racecourse in the world, two wildlife-rich lochs and an Iron Age fort.

'Peebles for pleasure' went the old saying, and there is certainly much of that in this superb ramble along the River Tweed from this attractive old border town.

The ruins of Kelso's abbey are just one of the highlights passed on this walk, which begins along an old railway and returns beside the river past the site of old Roxburgh and its castle.

From the attractive green in Denholm, the Borders Abbeys Way leads to the ancient hamlet of Bedrule. The return follows grassy field paths and woodland strips to shady Denholm Dean.

After leaving the historic burgh of Lauder by the Southern Upland Way, this walk joins the route of the Lauder Common Riding. Gradually climbing to the 1,240-foot (378-m) summit, it offers all-round views.

Starting close to Jedburgh Abbey, this walk crosses the historic Canongate Bridge then rises above the town. It uses parts of the Borders Abbeys Way and the Roman Road of Dere Street.

Sir Walter Scott's home, a delightful local beauty spot and a grand walk beside the River Tweed are combined on this ramble from a small loch on the edge of Galashiels.

The pub at Kirk Yetholm used to provide a free half pint to walkers completing the Pennine Way courtesy of Alfred Wainwright. This rewarding trek combines the two options for the last leg of that journey.

Set deep in the hills at the head of the Yarrow Valley, St Mary's Loch is the largest natural loch in Scottish Borders. This route circuits the loch, visiting Dryhope Tower and St Mary's Kirkyard.

The highest point on the eastern section of the Southern Upland Way lies across the flank of Minch Moor. It is combined here with a forest ramble and an easy finish along the valley of the River Tweed.

An ancient way called the Minchmoor Road runs up a grassy ridge to the crest of the hills, where the Southern Upland Way is met and followed to the tall cairns of the Three Brethren.

From Melrose Abbey, this walk follows the Southern Upland Way north over open farmland. It returns down Leader Water to the Leaderfoot Viaduct over the Tweed and Trimontium Roman fort.

Keymap

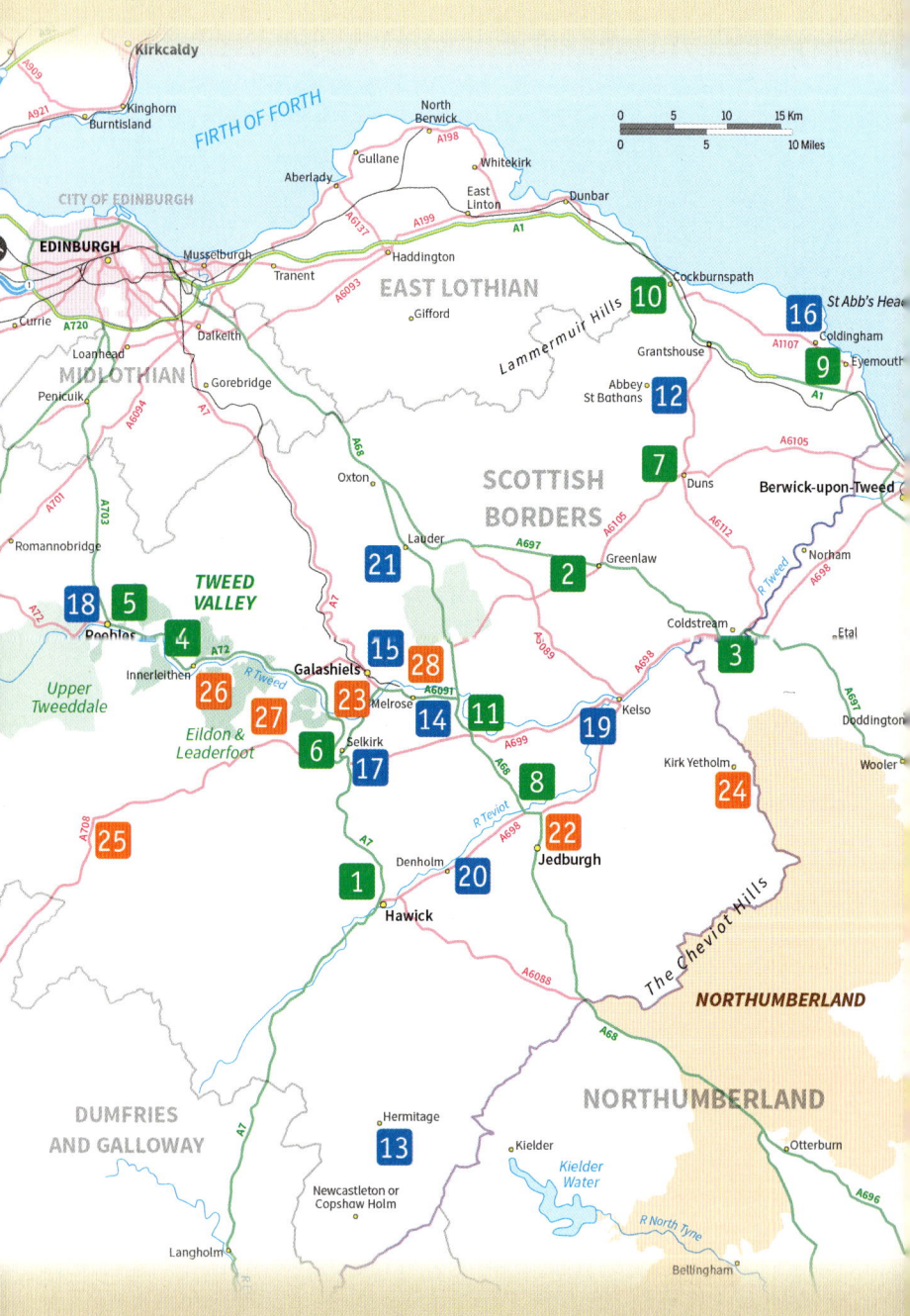

Introduction to Scottish Borders

The geography and history of Scottish Borders have combined to create a distinctive landscape with a unique culture. This region offers much fine walking with fascinating points of interest to explore at every turn.

The land under your feet
The Southern Uplands, which also span neighbouring Dumfries and Galloway to the west, extend across Scottish Borders. They are characterised by high hills with rounded summits and steep-sided valleys. The streams that rise in the uplands become substantial rivers that wind through lower, rolling hills and plains of fertile farmland before reaching the coast.

Southern Upland Way signpost (Walk 26)

The terrain is dissimilar to the rest of Scotland because the underlying bedrock differs from the predominately very hard metamorphic rock found further north. By contrast, the Southern Uplands are composed mainly of sedimentary rock and were formed by geological processes that started 500 million years ago in the Ordovician period. The continents that joined to form what are now England and Scotland collided, creating a region of uplift. As the oceanic plate separating them slid under the neighbouring continental shelf, vast quantities of marine sediments were piled up on the upper plate. These compressed into rock bands of shale, siltstone and greywacke.

During later Devonian and Carboniferous periods more sedimentary rocks of sandstone, limestone and mudstone were laid on top. Many of these deposits were later removed by erosion. Subsequent uplift and erosion by ice sheets carved out glacial valleys, which can be seen in the west of the region. As the climate warmed, glacial meltwaters deposited sand and gravel sheets in the valleys, forming the alluvial flood plains of today's rivers.

The highest summit in the Scottish Borders, Broad Law (840 feet/256m), is part of the extensive Tweedsmuir Hills, the second largest area of mountain plateau in Scotland after the Highlands.

The River Tweed and its many tributaries drain the Scottish Borders. The 97-mile-long (155km) river flows west to east with about 20 miles (32km) of its lower reaches forming the border between Scotland and England. Many of the major Borders towns have grown up on its banks: Peebles, Innerleithen, Kelso, Melrose and Coldstream. Other towns straddle significant tributaries; Hawick lies on the River Teviot, Selkirk on Ettrick Water, Jedburgh on Jed Water and Galashiels on Gala Water. In the Tweed's middle reaches at Melrose, it flows through the Eildon and Leaderfoot National Scenic Area, where the conical Eildon Hills rise above the river's confluence with Leader Water.

Layers of history

When exploring the Scottish Borders it becomes apparent that humans have occupied and shaped this land for millennia. Before people arrived, woodland would have covered the land – thick and boggy on the lower ground and thinning to scrub higher up. So it's hardly surprising that the earliest visible traces of early settlement and routes are on high ground, where it would have been easier to travel and clear land for farming. Around places such as Peebles and Innerleithen every summit seems to be crowned by a hillfort and hut circles pepper the slopes.

The Romans arrived in Britain in AD 43 and gradually moved north to establish their major fort, Trimontium, around AD 80. Situated by the River Tweed it was named after the triple peaks

Sunset behind the Eildon Hills

of the Eildon Hills, whose north peak has remains of a large Bronze Age settlement. Trimontium was occupied on and off for a century, but the Romans eventually deserted the region, unable to hold it against the local Iron Age tribes.

During medieval times the region was part of the Anglo-Saxon kingdom of Northumbria. The language was Old English, which later developed into Scots; Gaelic was never widely spoken here. When the power of Northumbrian kings declined following repeated Viking invasions, this area became part of Scotland, which had emerged as an independent sovereign state in the 9th century. During the 12th century, Scotland's King David I established abbeys in Kelso, Jedburgh, Melrose and Dryburgh. These became great seats of wealth and power, until their dissolution following the Protestant Reformation in 1560. Built by skilled stone masons, their atmospheric ruins exhibit magnificent architecture.

The border lands remained disputed territory between England and Scotland for several centuries. The Wars of Scottish Independence wreaked great destruction during the late 13th and early 14th centuries. Lawlessness became common, with bands of armed men on horseback raiding the farms and settlements of rival clans to steal livestock, burn homes and take hostages. The depredations of these Border Reivers led many landowners to build peel towers where they could defend their family and possessions. Their tower houses, most now ruined, are a distinctive feature of the landscape.

Life remained volatile in the 17th century, when religious and political divergence led to the Covenanter Wars. This region was one of the key battlegrounds and suffered badly during 'The Killing Time' when extrajudicial execution of any Covenanters caught in arms was permitted.

All these troubles fed a rich vein of legend and folklore, which was source material for several literary figures. The best known of these, Walter Scott, came from a Borders clan and spent his childhood absorbing local stories. He collected and published Scottish ballads before developing a highly successful career as a historical novelist with stories based on real people and events. His work did much to define and popularise Scottish identity. His home, Abbotsford, stands on the banks of the Tweed upstream from Melrose.

A vibrant culture

The Scottish Borders are a rural area where the rich countryside supports large estates and thriving towns. Farming has provided prosperity since the heyday of the abbeys, which grew rich from the wool trade. The many large rivers provided water power for grain mills and later, as weaving was industrialised, for textile mills. Tweed – cloth woven in natural colours and often used for sportsman's clothing – remains an important product of the region. The River Tweed also brings in significant income through salmon fishing; it is one of Scotland's finest venues for this expensive sport.

Horse riding is a major activity and one that has helped to keep old byways open and accessible for walkers. These routes include ancient drove roads over the hills, which were used to move livestock to market.

The wealth of the countryside promoted the development of substantial burgh towns, each with its own character, but all contain handsome stone buildings and strong communities with numerous independent shops, and some have their own local history museum.

The expansion of railways in the 19th century linked several Borders towns to Edinburgh and other cities. Although closed during the 1950s and 60s, many lines continue as footpaths and cycle routes.

Walking in the area

The region has a slightly drier, warmer and sunnier climate than most of Scotland, although there is still plenty of rain to keep the grass green. Birdlife is plentiful and observant walkers might also spot signs of foxes, badgers and otters.

This is a glorious area for walking and this selection has been chosen to take the reader through beautiful and varied countryside and to visit many places of historical interest. The region is crossed by several long-distance paths, including the Southern Upland Way, St Cuthbert's Way and the Borders Abbeys Way. These linear routes often form part of the walks in this guide, which are all circular, starting and ending at the same point.

Most of the walks start from towns and villages that have a range of accommodation and are well served by bus routes and, for Walks 15 and 23, beginning at Galashiels, by railway.

This book includes a list of waypoints alongside the description of the walk, so that you can enjoy the full benefits of gps should you wish to.

For more information about route navigation, improving your map reading ability, walking with a GPS and for an introduction to basic map and compass techniques, read Pathfinder® Guide *Navigation Skills for Walkers* by outdoor writer Terry Marsh (ISBN 978-0-319-09175-3). This title is available in bookshops and online at shop.ordnancesurvey.co.uk

Common elements in place names	
Several Scots words that feature in the local dialect appear frequently in place names in Scottish Borders:	
Hope	a small upland valley enclosed by green hills or ridges.
Haugh	a piece of level ground by the banks of a river.
Knowe	a knoll or hillock, often associated in folklore with fairies.
Law	a conspicuous, conical-shaped hill that usually stands in isolation.
Water	a large stream, which is generally intermediate in size between a burn and a river.

The pond, Gordon Community Woodland (Walk 2)

Short walks up to 2½ hours

walk 1

River Teviot and Wilton Lodge Park

Start: Hawick

Distance: 2¼ miles (3.7km)

Height gain: 80 feet (25m)

Approximate time: 1 hour

Route terrain: Tarmac paths through riverside parkland

Parking: Common Haugh car park, Victoria Road

OS maps: Landranger 79 (Hawick & Eskdale), Explorer 331 (Teviotdale South)

GPS waypoints:
- NT 500 146
- Ⓐ NT 494 146
- Ⓑ NT 492 145
- Ⓒ NT 490 142
- Ⓓ NT 486 139
- Ⓔ NT 491 141
- Ⓕ NT 493 144

Wilton Lodge Park is a tranquil place to stroll with grassy playing fields, mature trees and the wildlife-rich River Teviot. As well as being home to Hawick Museum, it is full of interest with plenty of information boards to explain the sights. The walk passes a walled garden, play park and café, as well as an ornamental fountain, Victorian-style bandstand and several memorial sculptures.

Leave the Common Haugh car park by the exit and walk to the left along Victoria Road, passing Hawick Community Hospital. Where the road bends right, at the gates to Wilton Lodge Park, keep ahead on the pavement between the pillars and into the park. Walk ahead on the wide tarmac path with the River Teviot below. Level with a footbridge Ⓐ, keep left, staying by the river.

At a grassy area, fork right to visit the Gilbert Davidson Fountain. Beyond it, turn right (just before a footbridge) to the area in front of Hawick Museum Ⓑ. Metal silhouette sculptures remember Hawick men who fought at Passchendaele in 1917. A war memorial stands by a stream and there is a small waterfall 50 yards upriver.

Cross the footbridge on your left over the stream. Keep ahead past two statues, to rugby union commentator Bill McLaren and motorcycle champion Jimmie Guthrie, and walk through the park with a wooded bank on your right. By a metal fingerpost, fork right for the walled garden. Turn left past the walled garden Ⓒ and beyond a brick pavilion turn left down steps, back to the tarmac path through the park.

The Zandra Elliot Bandstand

> **Wilton Lodge** Since 1910, this 18th-century mansion has been home to Hawick Museum, the oldest museum in Scottish Borders. It contains a War Memorial Room, which tells the story of Hawick's people during the wars through fascinating objects and audio-visuals. The museum's artefacts and works of art not only tell Hawick's history, but also include displays about ancient Egypt, archaeology and nature.

Continue to the right under large beech trees until meeting the river at a T-junction **D**. Turn left and follow the tarmac path downstream. Opposite Langlands footbridge **E**, you can detour left to visit the Bandstand and Boer War Memorial.

Keep ahead along the path on the near side of the river to a play park. Here go up steps on the right, past a **café** and across the McLaren Bridge over the river **F**. Turn left along the bank, with a view across to Hawick Museum. Cross back over the river at the next bridge **A** and turn right to retrace your steps to the car park.

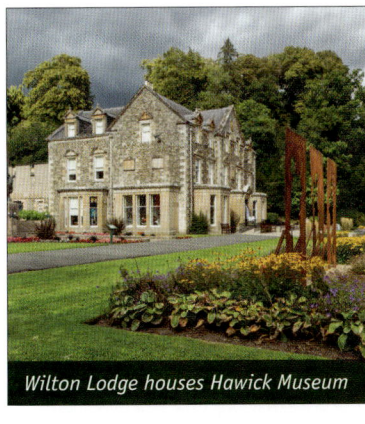

Wilton Lodge houses Hawick Museum

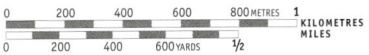

RIVER TEVIOT AND WILTON LODGE PARK • 11

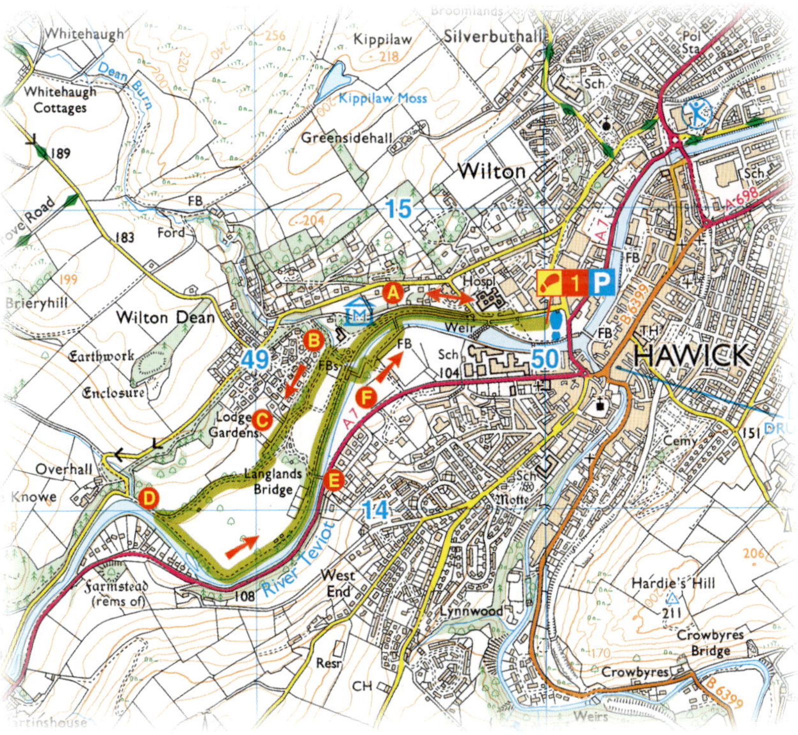

walk 2

Gordon Community Woodland

Start
Gordon Community Woodland

Distance
2¼ miles (3.5km)

Height gain
35 feet (10m)

Approximate time
1 hour

Route terrain
Paths through woodland and heathland

Parking
Gordon Community Woodland car park, entrance off A6105, just over ½ mile (900m) east of Gordon

OS maps
Landranger 74 (Kelso & Coldstream), Explorer 339 (Kelso, Coldstream & Lower Tweed Valley)

GPS waypoints
- NT 661 436
- Ⓐ NT 657 437
- Ⓑ NT 658 441
- Ⓒ NT 661 442
- Ⓓ NT 663 446
- Ⓔ NT 665 443

With a mix of broadleaved trees, Scots pine and open heathland, this is a delightful place for a stroll. Over 200 acres (80 hectares) in extent, the community woodland is relatively flat, which makes for easy walking along the network of paths. Red, blue and green trails are marked by posts with arrows. This woodland circuit combines these routes, visiting a prehistoric site, viewpoints and the pond.

The car park entrance is easiest to spot from the Gordon direction. It is just over ½ mile (900m) east of Gordon on the A6105. Turn left into the wood by a stone wall with a name plaque, 50 yards after a minor road junction on the right. From the east, it is a right turn 100 yards beyond a house on the edge of the wood.

👣 Facing the map board in the car park, go to your left along the all-abilities path. Curve right, ignoring steps over a wall on the left. Pass a picnic bench and continue until in sight of a footbridge, which leads to a track that runs into Gordon. Immediately before the bridge, turn right on a smaller path marked by a blue arrow Ⓐ.

The path meanders beside a wetland surrounding Eden Water, where herons and dragonflies may be seen. At another post, keep left by the stream with views out over farmland, ignoring right turns. Where a footbridge replaces a stone railway bridge, the path rises up to a bench that offers an elevated panorama Ⓑ.

Continue to the right along the disused railway line, soon entering an open area of heathland. The raised bumps on the left (shown as Cairns on the OS map) are Bronze Age burial mounds. At a post, a few yards before a blue arrow points right, turn left along a section of wooden boardwalk Ⓒ.

The path crosses a burn and runs straight ahead. It then trends right over more boardwalk and up to a bench in a broad glade. The path continues through this open corridor to a minor road Ⓓ.

Turn right and walk for 350 yards to a gravel parking area with another information board. Here, turn right on a path with a red arrow. This leads to a picnic bench by a pond. Go left on boardwalk that curves round the pond to a community cabin Ⓔ.

Continue past the shelter, now back on the disused railway

line. Keep straight ahead ignoring left turns. Just before reaching **C** turn left at a green arrow, passing between two metal posts with boardwalk underfoot initially. The path runs through young pines (look out for a willow stag under the trees). Where a path merges from the left, the surface becomes gravel. Keep ahead and the path soon curves right, back into the car park.

Gordon Community Woodland

When this woodland came up for sale in 2001, locals set up a community trust to purchase it, with assistance from the Scottish Land Fund. Their aim was to manage it sustainably for the benefit of people from Gordon village and beyond. Since then they have improved the structure of the wood and created access for recreation and education. The woodland is cared for by local volunteers.

Grassy path through an open glade

walk 3

Lees Haugh and Leet Water

Start
Coldstream

Distance
3¼ miles (5.2km)

Height gain
50 feet (15m)

Approximate time
1½ hours

Route terrain
Paved and well-surfaced paths and tracks; riverside embankment

Parking
Home Park car park, Court House Place, High Street

OS maps
Landranger 74 (Kelso & Coldstream), Explorer 339 (Kelso, Coldstream & Lower Tweed Valley)

GPS waypoints
- NT 840 396
- Ⓐ NT 838 394
- Ⓑ NT 838 391
- Ⓒ NT 844 388
- Ⓓ NT 851 386
- Ⓔ NT 845 395
- Ⓕ NT 840 395

The River Tweed takes a big loop on the edge of Coldstream round a flat and fertile plain called Lees Haugh. This is almost an island, as it is separated from the town by Leet Water, a stream that once powered mills. This walk offers fine views of the Tweed, where anglers can often be seen fishing for salmon. The route traces the southern border of Scotland; England lies on the other side of the river.

The riverside path after Ⓑ

From the car park, turn right past the Castle Hotel. Cross the road bridge over Leet Water and keep straight ahead. Opposite Woodlands Park, turn left between the pillars onto the drive at the gate lodge of Lees Park Ⓐ.

In about 75 yards fork right at a fingerpost onto a path that runs under trees. After a gap in a wall the path bends left down an avenue of young trees. Soon fork right and follow a fence round a field. When you see the Tweed, go left downhill to a grassy area then follow it down to the river. Turn left along the riverside path Ⓑ.

> **Penitent's Walk** As with nearby Nun's Walk, this path originates from Coldstream's 12th-century Cistercian Priory, which was founded as a nunnery in 1166. Nuns from the priory tended to the wounded after the Battle of Flodden in 1513 and used carts to retrieve the bodies of dead Scots nobles for burial in the grounds of the priory, which was near today's Market Square.

At a fingerpost bear right, staying on the riverside path. It soon bends left round the Stone Temple, where you join a gravel drive and continue to the right along it. At a sign, fork left onto a wooded path that avoids a fishing hut. On reaching a vast cultivated area, turn right between fields and woodland. This path climbs up onto the grassy water dyke, an embankment designed to keep floodwater off Lees Haugh, joining it beside a weir **C**.

Walk downstream with good views over the river, where anglers can often be seen fishing for salmon. Ignore a small path branching right and curve left on the grass bund past mature trees. Where the bund divides **D**, fork right, closer to the river.

White posts show the names of the various fishing beats. Continue downstream when the two bunds rejoin, now on a gravel track. Near the town you can see the Marjoribanks Monument, a statue on a tall column. The track bends left before Leet Water **E**.

Join a concrete track and keep ahead on it. Beyond a concrete ramp and before a barrier, fork right on a small path that leads to a footbridge over Leet Water. Cross over and immediately turn right along Penitent's Walk **F**.

Follow the paved path along an attractive water meadow beside Leet Water. When it meets Abbey Road near the Tweed, turn left up the road into the town centre. Bend left past Coldstream Museum then fork right past Market Square. Keep ahead to a crossroads and turn left along the High Street back to the car park.

Marjoribanks Monument

Charles Albany Marjoribanks was the MP for Berwickshire from 1832 until his death aged 39. During his short term as a Liberal representative he helped to pass the Reform Bill, which increased the number of people eligible to vote. The monument was constructed in 1834 and the statue was replaced after being struck by lightening in 1873.

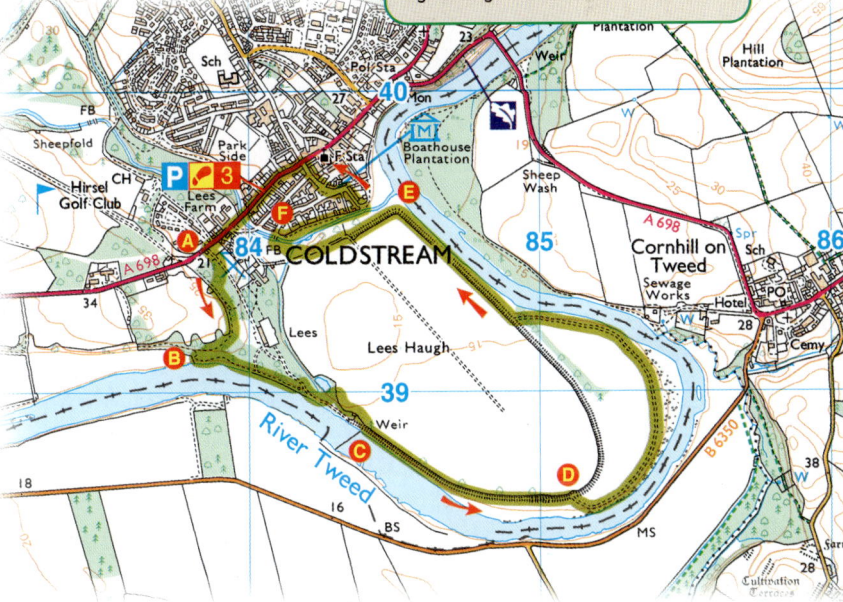

LEES HAUGH AND LEET WATER • 15

walk 4

Caerlee and the River Tweed

Start
Innerleithen

Distance
3½ miles (5.8km)

Height gain
360 feet (110m)

Approximate time
1¾ hours

Route terrain
Riverside tarmac path, good forest tracks and grassy hill paths

Parking
Hall Street car park

OS maps
Landranger 73 (Peebles, Galashiels & Selkirk), Explorer 337 (Peebles & Innerleithen)

GPS waypoints
 NT 328 367
Ⓐ NT 331 362
Ⓑ NT 313 370
Ⓒ NT 317 376
Ⓓ NT 324 369
Ⓔ NT 325 367

Starting with a gentle amble beside the River Tweed, this walk climbs gradually onto Caerlee Hill. It is a splendid viewpoint, offering a bird's-eye view of Innerleithen and the intersecting river valleys below. The route circuits the ring of prehistoric earthworks at the top of the hill, a defensive Iron Age settlement.

Walk down Hall Street to the main road and go straight across onto Traquair Road. Follow the road for 400 yards then turn right onto the Tweed Valley Railway Path Ⓐ, indicated by a blue sign on the opposite side of the road.

Stay on this tarmac path for 1⅓ miles (2.1km), passing occasional interpretation boards. The first is about large sheds beside the path, built as food stores in World War II. Ignore a cross path where the disused railway squeezes between road and river, and later pass National Tree Collections apple orchards. Turn right before a house at the blue sign for Innerleithen by Caerlee Bank Ⓑ.

Walk up towards farm buildings on the road. Cross with care and go right then immediately left up a track. Walk uphill past Velvet Hall Alpacas (who may peer at you curiously over the fence) to a junction Ⓒ and turn right, signed Innerleithen.

Contour along the hillside on a track through lovely oak and beech woodland. Fork right onto a lesser track at a post, where the main track bends left uphill. Cross a stream then fork left (right goes through a gate into a field). Gradually climb uphill through coniferous woodland until a gate and stile Ⓓ lead onto open hillside.

Don't go through the kissing-gate ahead (unless you want to avoid a stile), but turn right on a grassy path that circuits Caerlee Hill and has superb views over the Tweed Valley as it curves left. Go over a stile in the wall that runs over the crest of the hill and bear diagonally left. Cross a ruined wall on a small path that curves round the foot of the earthworks, with Innerleithen coming into view below. Just before a communications mast, fork right downhill on a grassy path Ⓔ (or for a gentler finish keep ahead and go down the tarmac track serving the communications mast).

Descend steeply through gorse and young trees to the track and turn right down the tarmac. It soon bends right and runs down to a wooden gate with a gap beside it. Descend to a bend on St Ronan's Terrace and go first left then first right back to the car park.

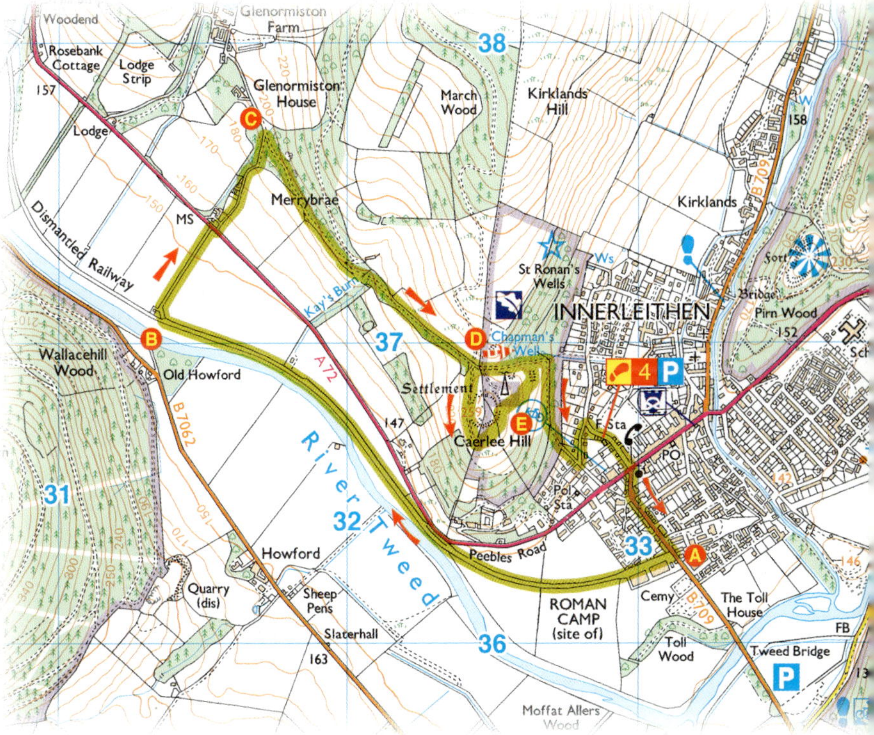

Grassy path descending Caerlee Hill

Tweed Valley Railway Path

This 5-mile/8-km long tarmac path links Innerleithen and Peebles via the course of a disused railway. When the line opened in 1864 it had a private halt at **B** for the use of the family and guests of Glenormiston House. The cottage here was built for a railway maintenance worker.

Caerlee Hillfort

The upstanding earthworks of a prehistoric defended settlement crown Caerlee Hill. The fort was probably occupied by Iron Age Celts and is mirrored by another on Pirn Hill to the north-east, on the other side of Leithen Water. Quarrying in the 19th century destroyed parts of the fort and uncovered bronze bracelets. The platforms for six buildings can still be traced inside.

CAERLEE AND THE RIVER TWEED • 17

walk 5

Ven Law and Soonhope

Start: Peebles

Distance: 3¾ miles (6km)

Height gain: 540 feet (165m)

Approximate time: 2 hours

Route terrain: Firm tracks and paths through forest and around the valley

Parking: East Station car park, Edinburgh Road

OS maps: Landranger 73 (Peebles, Galashiels & Selkirk), Explorer 337 (Peebles & Innerleithen)

GPS waypoints:
- NT 254 405
- **Ⓐ** NT 254 407
- **Ⓑ** NT 261 410
- **Ⓒ** NT 265 416
- **Ⓓ** NT 269 415
- **Ⓔ** NT 261 402
- **Ⓕ** NT 256 401

The bustling town of Peebles with its many independent shops is only a short walk away from tranquil Soonhope Glen, a haven of green pasture surrounded by woodland. Wildlife present includes voles, great spotted woodpeckers, buzzards, owls and kestrels. This walk curves round the prominent hill of Ven Law, which is scattered with the remains of several prehistoric settlements, evidence that the area has been well populated for millennia.

From the car park exit, go left along Edinburgh Road for 300 yards then turn up the first road on the right, Venlaw High Road. It bends right, and soon divides – take the left fork. Before the first houses, bear left on a broad track past a green sign for Venlaw Forest **Ⓐ**.

The track climbs into the forest then levels off and passes above a quarry. It bends left into Soonhope Glen and runs beside mature deciduous trees that line the bottom of the forest. Exit the trees by a wooden gate with a sign for Glenhield Kennels **Ⓑ**.

Keep ahead with lovely views over the glen to the chalets of Holiday Village, mainly built in the post-war period by ex-servicemen and their families. Just before a fork in the track, turn right at a fingerpost signed Peebles **Ⓒ** and go down stone steps and through a wooden gate.

Walk along a fenced path that curves left above the burn then dips down to a wooden gate, where you may hear ducks on the pond ahead. Turn right over a sleeper bridge across Soonhope Burn. Keep ahead, crossing a smaller stream by stepping stones, and walk uphill beside a forest with a field on your right. At the top, meet a track by a fingerpost **Ⓓ** and turn right for Peebles.

In 500 yards, pass through a gate and continue on the track, which curves left to pass the holiday chalets. Cross a burn by a concrete bridge then keep ahead on a road past houses in Soonhope until you reach the A72 **Ⓔ**.

Turn right along the pavement. At the first turning on the left, carefully cross the road and then go through a metal gate. Walk ahead on a path beside playing fields. The path bends right before a fence, giving a view up to Ven Law, with Peebles Hydro at its foot.

Peebles Hydro Hydropathic hotels, where guests drank and bathed in local waters for health cures, became very fashionable in the Victorian era. The original Peebles Hydro was a French Renaissance style building with many turrets. After it burned down the hotel was rebuilt to a different design in 1907. It served as a hospital during both World Wars.

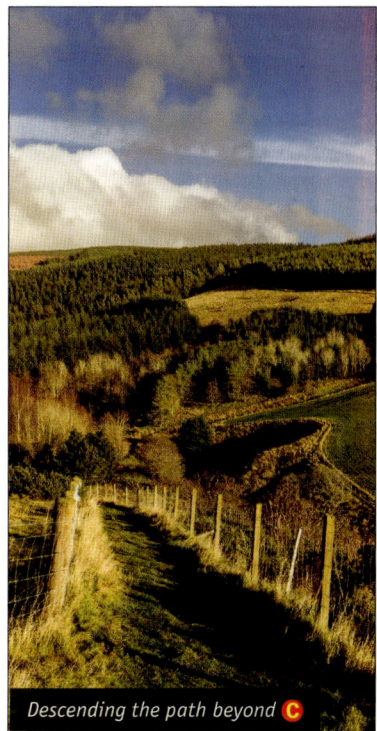

Descending the path beyond **C**

Where the path approaches the river **F**, turn right. Pass to the right of a leisure centre and walk through its car park. Just beyond an electricity substation, turn right up steps on a path that leads to the roundabout at the A72/A703 junction. Cross the road and follow Edinburgh Road (A703) back to the car park.

SCALE 1:25 000 or 2½ INCHES to 1 MILE 4CM to 1KM

0 200 400 600 800 METRES 1 KILOMETRES

0 200 400 600 YARDS ½ MILES

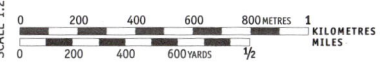

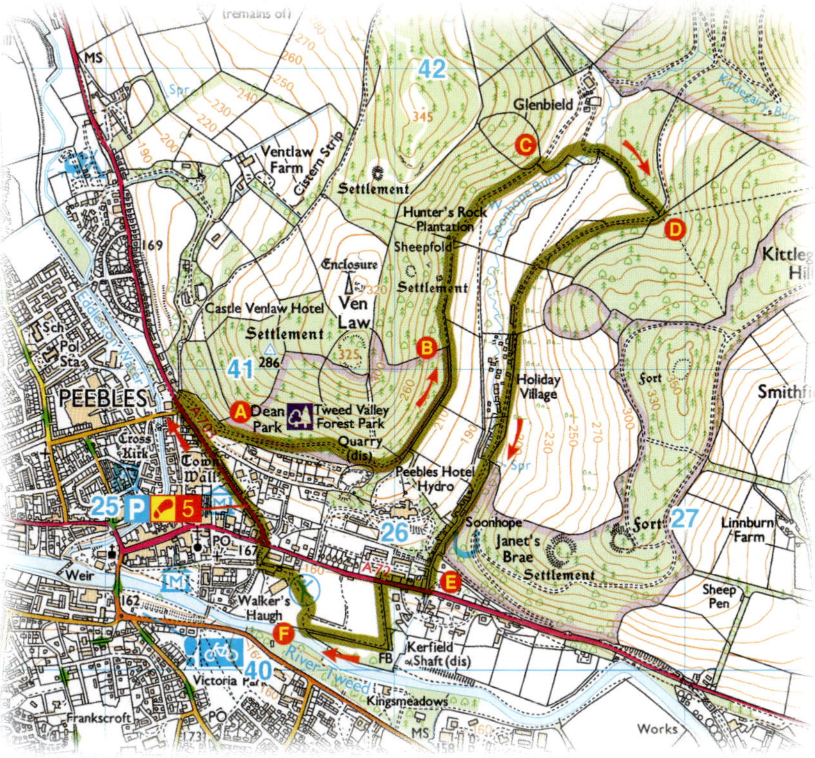

walk 6

Ettrick Water Circuit, Selkirk

Start
Selkirk

Distance
4¼ miles (7km).
Optional extension –
B-**C**-**B**: ⅔ mile (0.9km)

Height gain
55 feet (15m).
B-**C**-**B**: negligible

Approximate time
2 hours.
B-**C**-**B**: ½ hour

Route terrain
Tarmac path.
B-**C**-**B**: riverside and woodland track

Parking
Victoria Park car park

OS maps
Landranger 73 (Peebles, Galashiels & Selkirk), Explorer 338 (Galashiels, Selkirk & Melrose)

GPS waypoints
- NT 464 288
- **A** NT 459 282
- **B** NT 448 274
- **C** NT 445 273
- **D** NT 450 277
- **E** NT 462 285
- **F** NT 464 289
- **G** NT 470 295

This easy walk can be made even shorter by tackling only one of the two halves, downstream or upstream of Ettrick Bridge. Most of the walk is on tarmac paths, which feel surprisingly rural despite following the river through the historic town of Selkirk. Philiphaugh Estate has a salmon viewing centre, gardens and a café, conveniently situated just off the walk.

The southern part of this route follows the Salmon Leap Path, marked by posts with red arrows. The northern part has yellow arrows. The optional extension of ⅔ mile (0.9km) from the Cauld at **B** to the confluence of Yarrow Water with Ettrick Water at **C** is on riverside and woodland tracks, but the rest of the walking is on tarmac paths.

Leave the back of the car park and turn left on a tarmac path beside a grassy flood bank. At the end of playing fields bear left, uphill to the road (not on the Nature Trail signed ahead). Turn right along the pavement and then right over Selkirk Bridge. Take the first left and walk along Ettrickhaugh Road past Selkirk Rugby Club.

Where the houses on the left end, turn left and cross a footbridge **A**. The path bends right, but immediately fork left at a fingerpost down a path with steps. Walk through woodland to the riverbank and continue upstream. The steep bank on the far side is being dramatically eroded. About 120 yards after a broken weir, a red arrow indicates the path continuing on the field side of the riparian woodland. At a junction with a track, bear left back to the riverside. The path soon comes to the Cauld **B**, where a weir stretches across the river.

For the optional extension, continue past it on a track. At a crossroads with a path turn left and walk a short distance to the confluence of Ettrick and Yarrow waters, both substantial rivers **C**. *Return along the path to the crossroads and go straight over, later emerging from the woodland to rejoin the track just before arriving back at the Cauld* **B**.

Stay on the track then fork left onto a tarmac path beside the lade (channel). In 400 yards, a footbridge **D** crosses to Philiphaugh Salmon Viewing Centre and the popular **Watermill Café**.

Continue on the path, which soon drops down to run right beside the water. The field on the other side was the site of the Battle of Philiphaugh in 1645, where Royalists defeated a

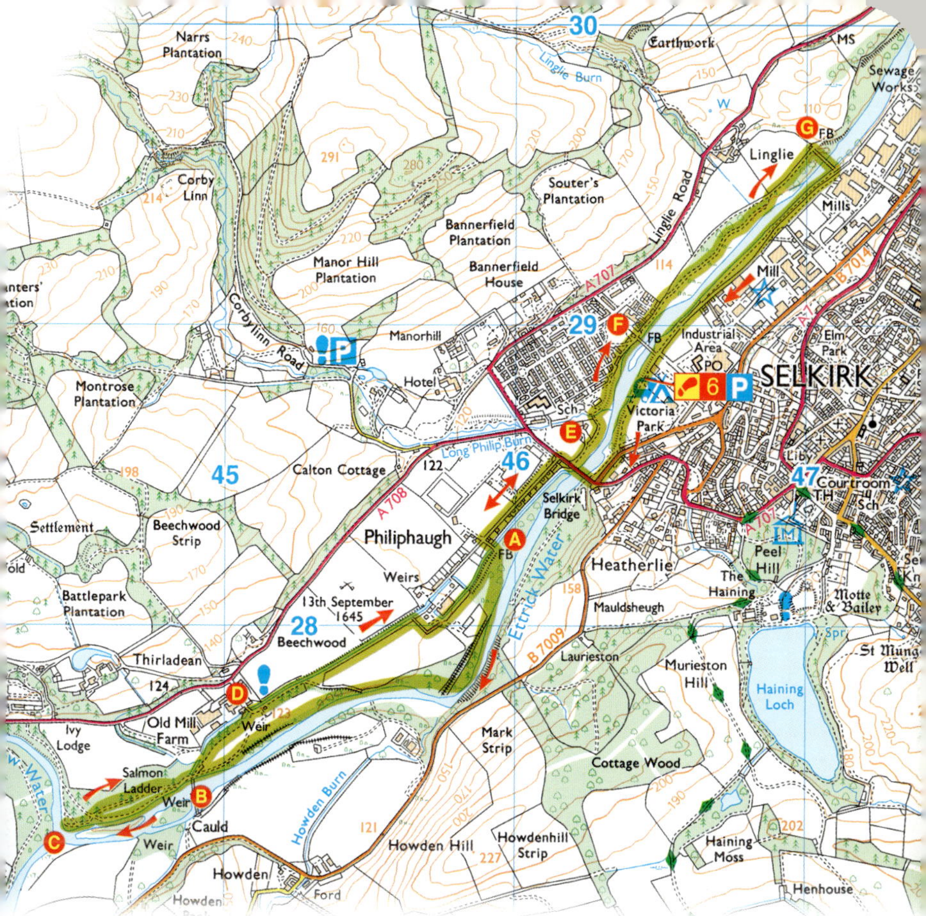

Covenanter army. Just before a disused fish farm the path goes right then left. It then runs straight to the footbridge at **A**. Cross over and return along Ettrickhaugh Road then turn right. Before the bridge, turn left by a white sign for Matt Fuels. Where the lane bends left, keep ahead on a tarmac path marked by a yellow arrow **E**.

Soon cross a footbridge over Long Philip Burn and turn right at the T-junction beyond. Keep ahead past a stylish footbridge **F** (a possible shortcut). The path soon enters woodland.

The second footbridge across the river **G** is about ⅔ mile (900m) beyond the first. Here the path bends right over a long white metal bridge, which initially crosses a wooded island. On the far side, turn right to return on the riverside path, ignoring other paths branching to the left. Pass a flood wall with mosaic images on it. Not far beyond the earlier footbridge, turn left back into Victoria Park.

0 200 400 600 800 METRES 1 KILOMETRES
0 200 400 600 YARDS ½ MILES

SCALE 1:25000 or 2½ INCHES to 1 MILE 4CM to 1KM

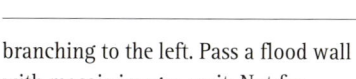

The Cauld Constructed by Sir John Murray of Philiphaugh in 1856, the Cauld comprised a weir across Ettrick Water and a geared sluice gate that directed water into a lade (artificial waterway). The flow turned a large waterwheel, which can still be seen at **D**. This powered a sawmill and adjacent threshing shed. In 2013, the Cauld was repaired and Archimedes screw turbines installed to generate electricity. The design incorporated a salmon pass.

walk 7

Hen Poo and Duns Castle

Start
Duns

Distance
4¼ miles (6.8km)

Height gain
375 feet (115m)

Approximate time
2 hours

Route terrain
Pavement; estate drive; grassy and woodland paths

Parking
Market Square (max. 2 hours) or car park at south end of Murray Street (NT 786 538)

OS maps
Landrangers 67 (Duns, Dunbar & Eyemouth) or 73 (Peebles, Galashiels & Selkirk), Explorer 346 (Berwick-upon-Tweed)

GPS waypoints
- NT 785 538
- Ⓐ NT 783 542
- Ⓑ NT 784 545
- Ⓒ NT 780 550
- Ⓓ NT 779 551
- Ⓔ NT 774 551
- Ⓕ NT 776 534

The old Scottish burgh of Duns has a long and turbulent history, but is now an attractive small town surrounded by peaceful countryside. This walk circuits the designed landscape of Duns Castle and includes a there-and-back climb to a prehistoric fort. It passes wildlife-rich Hen Poo, a lake which is much more picturesque than it sounds, its name being a corruption of Heron Pool.

From the Market Cross, walk up the right-hand side of Market Square and continue ahead up Castle Street. On meeting the A6105, cross over with care and continue uphill. When the road bends right, keep straight ahead, still on Castle Street. At the top walk through the entrance archway of Duns Castle estate Ⓐ.

In 50 yards turn right up steps, signed for Duns Law Fort (or omit this climb and save ¾ mile/1.2km and 180 feet/55m of ascent). Follow the path fairly steeply up a woodland strip. At a fingerpost by a fence corner, fork right uphill then leave the wood by a gate. The fort occupies the broad hilltop surrounded by grassy earthworks and offers superb views in three directions. Walk diagonally left to the Covenanters' Stone then head east for the view and follow the bank of earthworks round to the south and the viewpoint indicator and bench Ⓑ, overlooking Duns. From here you can see Lindisfarne and Bamburgh Castle on the coast of England and the Cheviot Hills round to Carter Bar. Return down the woodland path to Ⓐ.

Continue to the right along the estate drive to a memorial cairn to John Duns Scotus, an influential philosopher and theologian, who was born here in 1266. Turn right, before castellated Pavilion Lodge, which spans an archway. After crossing a cattle grid, Hen Poo comes into view. Beyond another cattle grid fork left, leaving the tarmac for a woodland track Ⓒ.

The track bends left round the end of the lake to a T-junction. Go left then, in 100 yards, turn right onto St Mary's

> **Duns Castle** The Earl of Moray, King Robert the Bruce's nephew, erected Duns Castle in the 14th century. It has been the seat of the Hay family since 1696 and successive generations have enlarged and embellished the tower house. The grand edifice is set in parkland on the edge of estate woodland and Hen Poo is part of a nature reserve.

> **Duns Law** This prominent hill is composed of old red sandstone that protrudes above softer greensand. The wide, sheep-grazed summit has multiple earthworks that are the remains of an Iron Age fort and settlement. A cairn marks where a Covenanter army raised their standard in 1639. They assembled here under the command of Sir Alex Leslie and their encampment added to the hilltop earthworks.

Duns Castle

Glade **D**. This path winds gently uphill, passing through open grassland to a track junction. Go left then left again at a T-junction with a larger track **E** and walk south towards the A6105.

Stay on the woodland track, ignoring side turnings. After passing a stone cottage in an open field, turn right at a crossroads of tracks. Join a drive by some castle outbuildings and bear right along it. Soon there is a good view leftwards over parkland to Duns Castle. Keep ahead at a junction.

At the main road **F**, turn left along the pavement with schools on both sides. After passing the old Duns Primary School, fork right and keep ahead back to the Market Square.

HEN POO AND DUNS CASTLE • 23

walk 8 — *Peniel Heugh*

Start: Harestanes Visitor Centre, 1 mile (1.6km) east of Ancrum

Distance: 4½ miles (7.4km)

Height gain: 625 feet (190m)

Approximate time: 2¼ hours

Route terrain: Lanes, tracks and woodland paths

Parking: Harestanes Visitor Centre car park

OS maps: Landranger 74 (Kelso & Coldstream), Explorer OL16 (The Cheviot Hills)

GPS waypoints:
- 🖉 NT 641 244
- Ⓐ NT 644 246
- Ⓑ NT 647 254
- Ⓒ NT 653 263
- Ⓓ NT 645 265
- Ⓔ NT 638 258
- Ⓕ NT 644 248

The circuit climbs to the stunning viewpoint of Peniel Heugh, where a striking monument remembers the Battle of Waterloo. A roundabout return through woodland and along quiet lanes eventually joins St Cuthbert's Way, passing a delightful walled garden before returning to Harestanes.

🖉 Go back out of the car park and head left to the end of the track. There turn left, abandoning the drive after 100 yards for a parallel path behind the trees on the left. Curve with it round the field corner to cross a plank bridge, briefly accompanying the stream before swinging up steps onto a wider path Ⓐ.

Follow it left into woodland, soon passing a small wildlife pond. Keep ahead past a junction, shortly meeting a tarmac drive. To the right is Monteviot House, seat of the marquesses of Lothian, whose gardens are open to the public. The route, however, rises left to a road, continuing along the drive opposite. Approaching the gamekeeper's house, fork right onto a grass track, going right again after 50 yards onto a narrower path climbing at the edge of trees to a lane Ⓑ.

Go right and almost immediately left onto a rising woodland trail. Keep left at successive forks, higher up being rewarded with a sudden glimpse of the summit tower. Bear left, staying within the trees and soon reaching a gate out of the wood. A contained path leads to a second gate, beyond which, turn right beside the fence to the top of the hill Ⓒ.

Drop north onto a grass track that leads away to the right.

> **Waterloo Monument**
> Rising 150 feet (45m), the monument was erected by the sixth Marquess of Lothian to commemorate the Duke of Wellington's victory at Waterloo.

The Waterloo Monument on Peniel Heugh

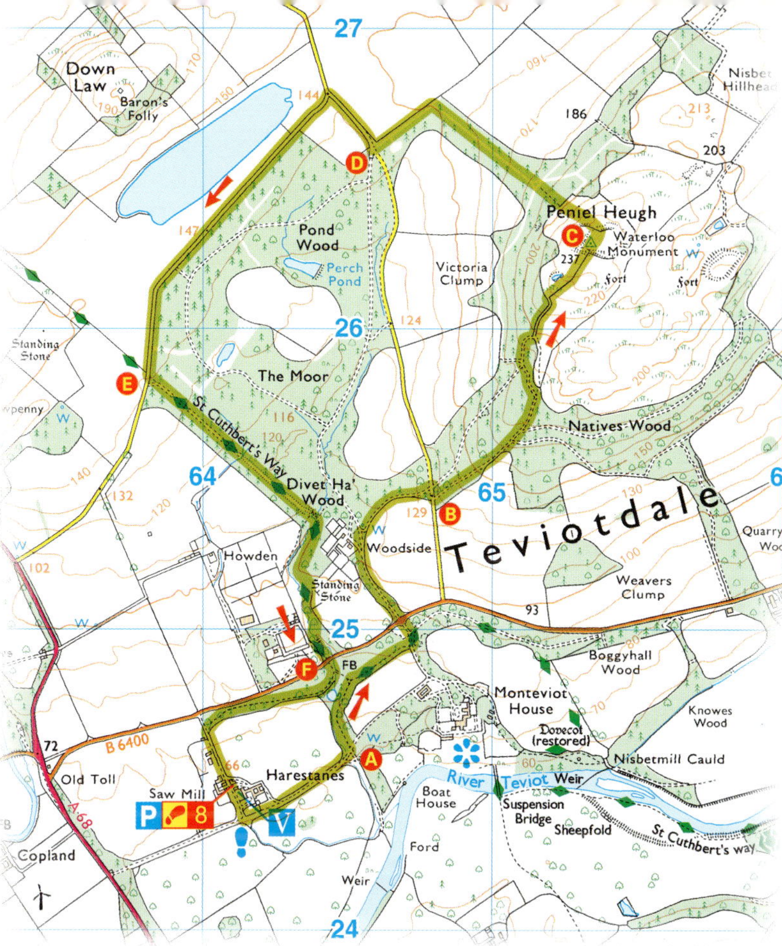

0 200 400 600 800 METRES 1 KILOMETRES
MILES
0 200 400 600 YARDS ½

SCALE 1:25000 or 2½ INCHES to 1 MILE 4CM to 1KM

Passing through a broken wall, immediately turn left on a trod that falls steeply below the wall towards the forest. Over a stile, a path descends steadily through the trees. Eventually meeting a track, go left out to a lane **D**.

Turn right to a junction and go left onto a long, straight lane. Crossing a bridge a few yards along, there is a fine view back to the hill, while farther on, a small loch to the right attracts geese, swans and other waterbirds. Follow the lane for 3/4 mile (1.2km) then, shortly beyond a bend, look for a gap in the left wall **E**.

Marked St Cuthbert's Way, a path heads into the thick of the trees, its almost dead-straight course betraying Roman origins. It is in fact Dere Street, which ran for almost 200 miles (320km) between York and the Firth of Forth. In time, the way swings over a bridge spanning a stream. Ignore the crossing path and keep going above the burn, eventually crossing it again at a second bridge. A signpost just beyond invites a detour to **Woodside Walled Garden**, where the **tearoom** uses local produce for its appetising range of snacks and light meals.

Return to follow St Cuthbert's Way down to the road, crossing to the continuing path opposite. Approaching a bridge **F**, turn right to remain on this bank. A pleasant path winds through old woodland dominated by ancient beech, and finally swings left to the Harestanes Visitor Centre.

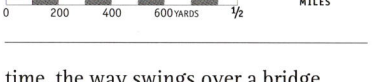

walk 9

Eyemouth Fort and Pocklaw Slap

Start
Eyemouth

Distance
4½ miles (7.2km)

Height gain
330 feet (100m)

Approximate time
2¼ hours

Route terrain
Tarmac, gravel and grassy paths along cliffs, field paths and pavement

Parking
Parking at the seaward end of Harbour Road

OS maps
Landranger 67 (Duns, Dunbar & Eyemouth), Explorer 346 (Berwick-upon-Tweed)

GPS waypoints
- NT 946 643
- Ⓐ NT 942 645
- Ⓑ NT 943 649
- Ⓒ NT 940 650
- Ⓓ NT 936 646
- Ⓔ NT 924 652
- Ⓕ NT 945 642

As it leads out of Eyemouth towards distant St Abb's Head, the Berwickshire Coastal Path offers easy clifftop walking with tremendous views. On The Bantry, Eyemouth's promenade, it passes the poignant *Widows and Bairns* sculpture that remembers the families left behind when 129 Eyemouth fisherman were drowned in 1881 by a powerful and unexpected storm. The route visits the earthworks and cannons of Eyemouth Fort and returns along an ancient track, Pocklaw Slap. Care is needed close to the unfenced cliffs.

Start outside The Contented Sole, a bar/restaurant at the junction of Harbour Road, Marine Parade and St Ella's Court. The large Georgian building on the far side of the harbour is Gunsgreen House. Walk towards the harbour mouth and opposite the modern harbour building go left along the seafront promenade, which is called The Bantry.

Where the promenade ends in front of Eyemouth Leisure Centre Ⓐ, go right onto the beach, as signed for the Coastal Path. Walk along it for 100 yards then go left up a flight of

> **Gunsgreen House** Built in 1753, this imposing house was the home of John Nisbet, who maintained a front as a respectable merchant, but who made his fortune as a smuggler. He employed John Adam, from the family of famous architects, to design the house. It has enormous cellars for storing contraband, such as brandy, tea and tobacco, which were highly taxed if imported legally.

Gunsgreen House

Coastal Path with St Abb's Head in the distance

steps to the caravan park. At the top, go right along the coastal path then turn right, signed Eyemouth Fort. Pass an information board and keep ahead to cannons on the point at **B**.

Continue round the other side of the headland then bear left through a dip back to the path and go right, past the information board. Turn right to continue along the coastal path. At a fingerpost by an entrance to the caravan park, go diagonally right across grass and through a gap in a low wooden fence onto a headland above the jagged rocks of Hairy Ness **C**.

Enjoy a fine view to St Abb's Head then continue round the point, forking right to follow the cliffs with care. Pass a fingerpost and continue right along

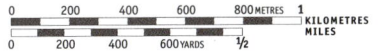

EYEMOUTH FORT AND POCKLAW SLAP • 27

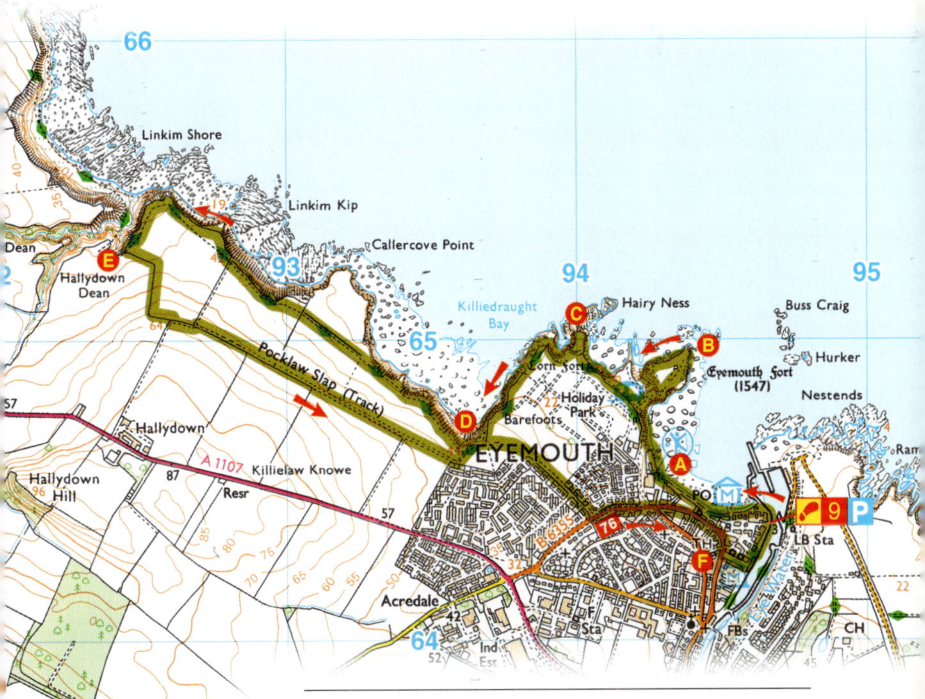

> **Eyemouth Fort**
>
> This was the first Trace Itallienne (on Italian lines) fortification in Britain. Occupying a cliff-girt peninsula, it was built and occupied twice between 1547 and 1559, first by English then by French troops (the latter were allies of the Scots). This was the era when gunpowder and cannons first came into use. Now that stone castle walls could be blown apart, a different design was required. So it was constructed with thick earth banks, with gaps for cannons to fire through, and projecting bastions.

the well-signed Coastal Path, which is diverted in places round crumbling cliffs. At the head of Killiedraught Bay the path rises up to a fingerpost **D** and bends right along the cliffs. (For a shortcut return, go sharp left here).

The path runs north-west for nearly 1 mile (1.6km), following the cliffs except at the broad headland of Callercove Point. It passes a blocky sea stack before bending left beside an old stone wall towards Hallydown Dean. Just before the path passes through two fence posts and drops down to the shore, turn left by a wall **E**. Walk up the left side of the wall, along the edge of the big field you've just skirted.

Keep left along the top of the field when the wall ends. At a gap, go right into the adjacent field and continue in the same direction. In 100 yards, go through another gap to keep ahead with the field boundary on your right. On reaching bungalows, turn left along the edge of a cultivated field back to the fingerpost at **D**. Here, fork right with a rose hedge on your left.

Join a residential road called Pocklaw Slap and keep ahead on the pavement. At a T-junction turn left onto the B6355 and walk down into the centre of Eyemouth, passing the Bantry car park. Follow the road as it narrows and slowly curves right. At a square with benches **F**, turn left past the museum, housed in a large stone building with a clock tower. At the next T-junction go left and walk back to the start with the harbour on your right. ●

The **Widows and Bairns** *sculpture remembers those left when 129 Eyemouth fishermen died in a storm in 1881*

Cockburnspath and Cove

walk

Start
Cockburnspath

Distance
5 miles (8km)

Height gain
510 feet (155m)

Approximate time
2½ hours

Route terrain
Well-marked paths through woods and along clifftops; quiet road

Parking
The Square, Cockburnspath

OS maps
Landranger 67 (Duns, Dunbar & Eyemouth), Explorer 346 (Berwick-upon-Tweed)

GPS waypoints
- NT 774 711
- Ⓐ NT 766 716
- Ⓑ NT 769 721
- Ⓒ NT 766 718
- Ⓓ NT 771 723
- Ⓔ NT 781 716
- Ⓕ NT 789 708
- Ⓖ NT 781 712

This walk starts at a cross erected by James IV of Scotland in 1503 in celebration of his marriage to Princess Margaret Tudor (the sister of Henry VIII), to whom he gave the lands of Cockburnspath. It visits well-preserved Dunglass Collegiate Church then descends a shady valley before a delightful stroll along clifftops past the historic fishing harbour of Cove. The walk finishes by following the final section of the Southern Upland Way back to Cockburnspath.

Facing the plaque on the cross in The Square, go right, up a narrow, walled lane. Pass the community shop and school then, when the road bends left, keep straight ahead on a footpath signed John Muir Way to Dunbar. Go through the gate into a wildlife conservation area and walk along the bottom of a wood with lovely views on the right to the sea. Torness nuclear power station shines white about 3 miles (5km) up the coast.

Leave the trees by a gate and keep ahead, contouring across a field towards wooded Dunglass Dean. Go through a gate with a sign for the Forth to Farne Way to a T-junction with a fingerpost Ⓐ. Turn right, downhill, on the John Muir Way.

On meeting a road at the bottom, turn left across a road bridge over Dunglass Burn. Immediately turn left on a drive between pillars by a lodge house and a sign for the Dunglass Collegiate Church Ⓑ. Alternatively, omit the ruins and turn right on the John Muir Way.

Walk up the wooded drive then bear left across grass to the doorless ruined church, which has interpretation boards inside Ⓒ. Return down the drive to Ⓑ, go straight across the road and under a railway viaduct. Turn right at a footpath sign onto a path that passes under the flyover carrying the A1 road over the wooded gorge.

At a track junction beyond a wooden barrier, turn right over Dunglass Old Bridge Ⓓ, leaving the John Muir Way. Join a tarmac lane and continue ahead to a roundabout. Turn left for Cove and Pease Bay, crossing over to walk on the pavement.

At a 'Cove (only)' sign, turn left down a minor road into the village. The road bends right to a small car park with information boards and a memorial to the 11 fishermen from

Cove who drowned in the 1881 Eyemouth Disaster. Keep straight ahead, ignoring the steep lane that leads down to Cove harbour.

Soon pass a wooden gate and fork left on a narrow path through shrubs to the clifftop. The soft sandstone cliffs erode easily and grass and wildflowers colonise the sloping debris. At an information board **E** keep ahead above the cliffs *or for a shortcut return, turn right for Cockburnspath and at Cove Farm go diagonally across a track junction down to the road at* **G**. Both directions are signed Southern Upland Way.

The path runs outside the fenced fields and above vegetated cliffs, where butterflies and bees flit between flowers in summer. At another information board there is a view of Cove harbour and various rock formations below. The path bends right at Hawk's Heugh, bringing the red sands of Pease Bay into view. Just beyond a kissing-gate at Old Linhead, meet a tarmac lane by a fingerpost **F** and turn right.

Walk up the lane for ½ mile (800m) to Cove Farm **G**. Before the roadside cottage (on the right), turn left at a post

> ### Dunglass Collegiate Church
>
> Founded in the 1440s by Sir Alexander Home, this church was dedicated to St Mary. It was a private chapel where a college of priests offered up perpetual prayers on behalf of the Home family. The cross-shaped building is remarkably well preserved and has intricate carved stonework inside. In medieval times Dunglass Castle and a market town stood nearby, but only the church remains. It was disestablished during the Protestant Reformation of 1560. In 1710, it passed to the Hall family, who used it as a stable and coach house.

with Forth to Farne and Southern Upland Way symbols and walk in front of a row of sandstone cottages. Keep ahead on the grassy path that goes under the railway line. Follow Southern Upland Way signs to the right, under the A1, and bend sharp left on a track. Curve right at a junction and continue to a gate onto a road. Turn left to the war memorial, which is the official end of the Southern Upland Way. Here turn right, following the road up to The Square and cross.

View from the wildlife conservation area

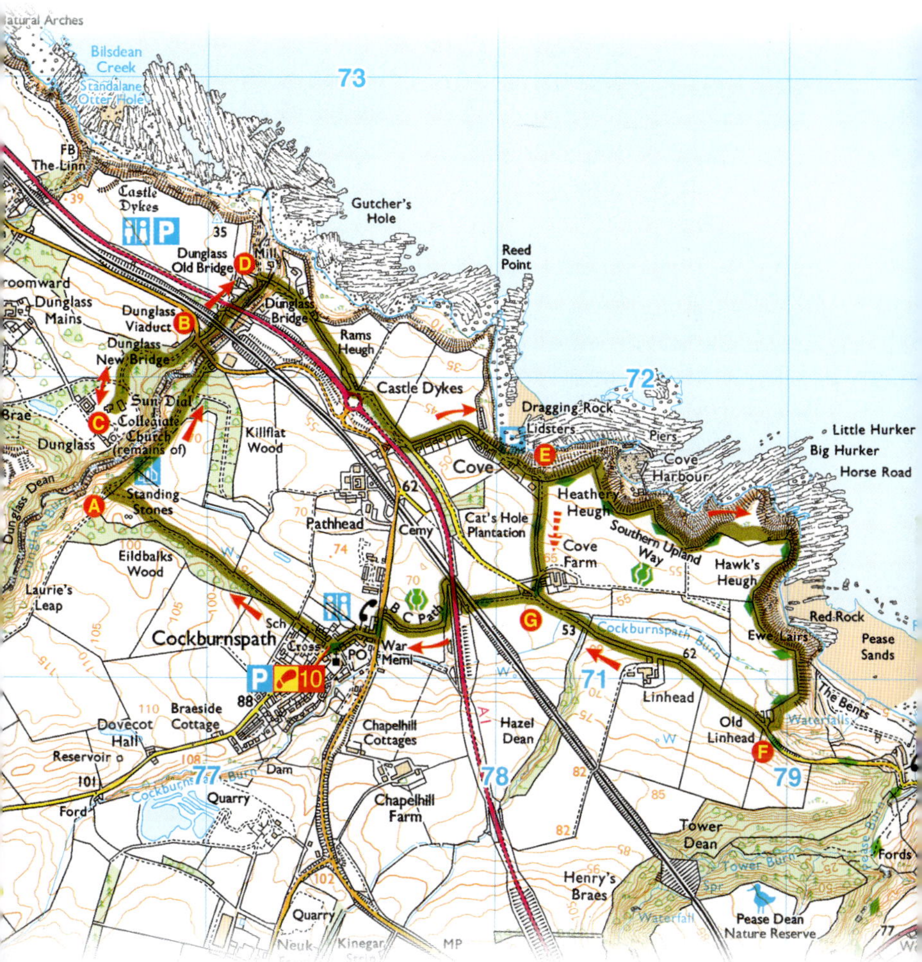

0 200 400 600 800 METRES 1 KILOMETRES
0 200 400 600 YARDS ½ MILES

SCALE 1:25000 or 2½ INCHES to 1 MILE 4CM to 1KM

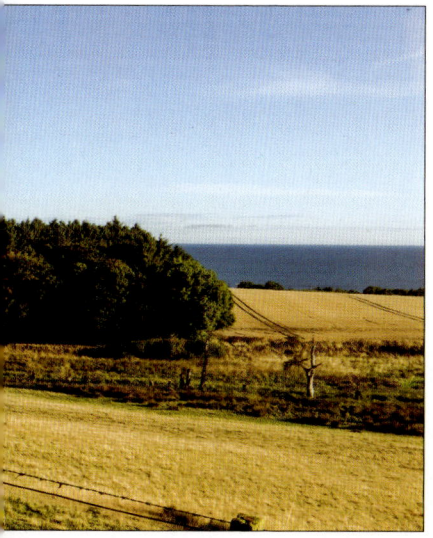

Southern Upland Way

Opened in 1984, the Southern Upland Way was Britain's first official coast-to-coast long-distance route. It runs from Portpatrick on the west coast through Dumfries and Galloway and Scottish Borders to Cove on the east coast, and terminates in Cockburnspath. The challenging route is 214 miles (344km) long and crosses over 80 hills that rise above 2,000 feet/610m. The final section met on this walk is one of its gentlest parts.

walk 11

St Boswells, Dryburgh and the River Tweed

Start
St Boswells

Distance
5 miles (7.9km)

Height gain
440 feet (135m)

Approximate time
2½ hours

Route terrain
Riverside paths, initially rough then with easier going

Parking
Car park behind bus terminus in St Boswells

OS maps
Landranger 74 (Kelso & Coldstream), Explorer 338 (Galashiels, Selkirk & Melrose)

GPS waypoints
- NT 593 309
- Ⓐ NT 592 311
- Ⓑ NT 588 313
- Ⓒ NT 588 320
- Ⓓ NT 593 316
- Ⓔ NT 603 323
- Ⓕ NT 609 320
- Ⓖ NT 595 315

Step back in time on this walk, which passes Dryburgh Abbey, founded in the 12th century, and a landscaped parkland created two hundred years ago. The route follows both banks of the River Tweed, which carves wide bends through woodland and pasture. It starts in St Boswells, a picturesque village named after Saint Boisil, an Abbot of Melrose.

> **Dryburgh Abbey** These graceful ruins are in the care of Historic Environment Scotland and are open all year (entry fee payable). The abbey was established by Premonstratensian canons from Alnwick Priory in 1150. Monastic life was brought to an end by the Protestant Reformation of 1560. The 11th Earl of Buchan created the designed landscape around the ruins and was buried here, as was Sir Walter Scott in 1832.

This walk follows St Cuthbert's Way, which is marked by the symbol of a white cross, along the south bank of the Tweed. On the north bank it uses the Borders Abbeys Way, whose logo is the letters W and A combined. The first ½ mile (800m) has slip and trip hazards before the path becomes easier going beyond Ⓑ.

From the bus terminus, turn left on the B6404 then first right along Hamilton Place, by a sign for St Cuthbert's Way. At

The Eildon Hills from Mertoun Bridge

a T-junction turn right then in 30 yards go left by a post with a yellow arrow and white cross. The path descends a steep stream valley and crosses a footbridge over it at the bottom **A**.

The path leads upstream beside the River Tweed. It undulates up and down with several flights of steps and sections of boardwalk. Take care as the wood can be slippery. The path descends to rocks on the edge of the river then crosses a footbridge over another side stream below The Holmes **B**. Here the path flattens out and the going becomes much easier.

The red sandstone building on the opposite bank is the Dryburgh Abbey Hotel. Dryburgh Abbey is adjacent to it but remains screened by trees. Keep left as the path follows a bend in the river to a green suspension footbridge **C**.

Cross the bridge, now leaving St Cuthbert's Way behind and picking up the Borders Abbeys Way, which bends right on the opposite bank. The Temple

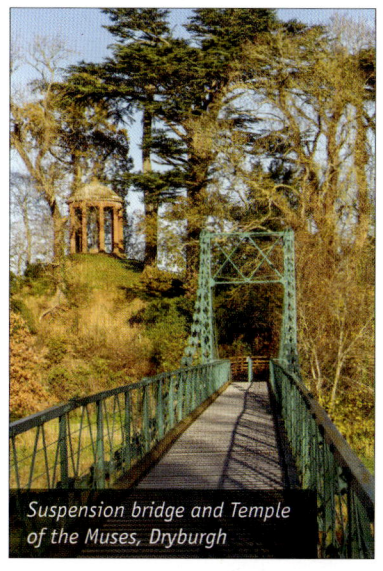

Suspension bridge and Temple of the Muses, Dryburgh

SCALE 1:25 000 or 2½ INCHES to 1 MILE 4CM to 1KM

0 200 400 600 800 METRES 1 KILOMETRES

0 200 400 600 YARDS ½ MILES

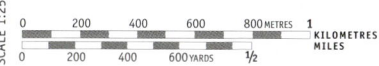

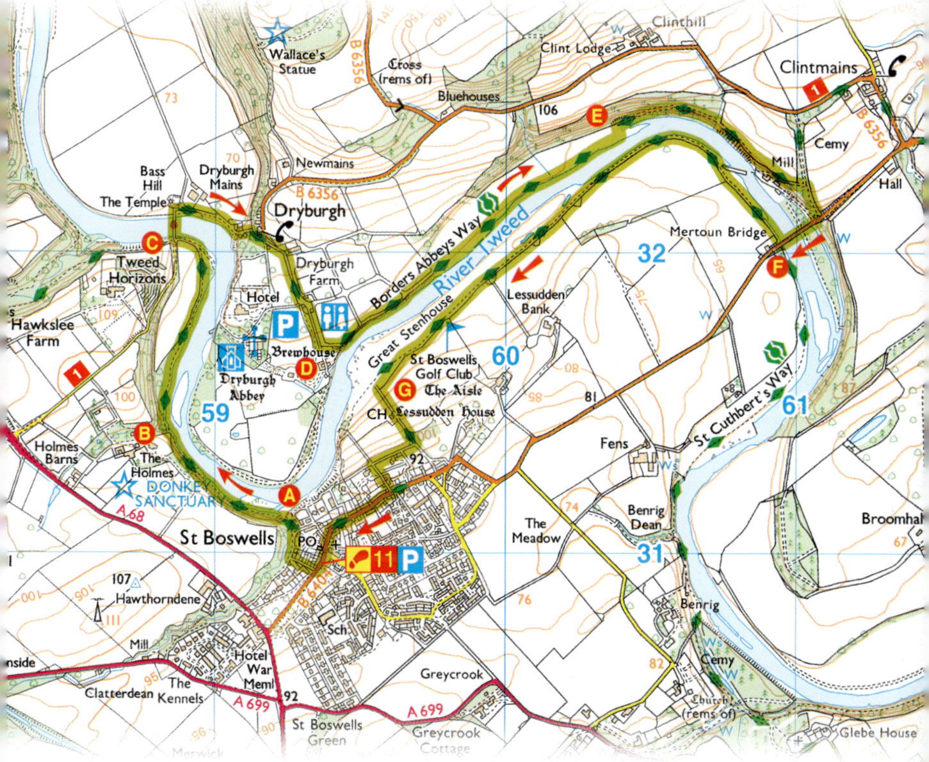

of the Muses stands on a knoll on the far side and can be accessed by a path on the left. Pass Dryburgh Farmhouse then Stirling Tower, white-washed cottages with a round turret on the end.

Walk up the minor road and go straight over a crossroads at the top. Pass Dryburgh Abbey car park and keep left of a house to go down a track. About 100 yards before the river, turn left at a Borders Abbeys Way sign by a gate and a stile **D**.

Walk past a walled garden and continue above the Tweed, with open views on the left over fields to a wooded hill. Initially willows line the river, but further on the path runs along its grassy bank with the manicured fairways of St Boswells Golf Club on the opposite side. Before the river bends to the right, the path leaves the bank and joins a track **E** that goes diagonally uphill.

When the track bends left, keep ahead through a gate into a sheep field and walk along its bottom edge. At the far end, go through a kissing-gate and bear left up to a fingerpost. Turn right, signed Mertoun Bridge (the Borders Abbeys Way goes left). The path runs under mature oaks then goes down steps to a road. Go right, across the bridge, enjoying a superb view to the three peaks of the Eildon Hills.

On the west bank, immediately turn right down steps with the St Cuthbert's Way logo **F** to a path beside the river. Now you can see the mill and weir you walked above and, beyond them, the sheer, eroded riverbank below the sheep field. The path follows the river round a bend. At St Boswells golf course, keep ahead on a path beside a fence with the fairways and river on your right.

When you come to a track **G**, turn left up it. At the top of a steep rise, turn right at a junction, now walking on the level. Walk past the high wall of a large old house. When the tarmac bends left, follow the lane to join the main road. There go right along the pavement back through the village to the start. ●

> **Wallace's Statue** This colossal monument to the Scottish hero is situated ½ mile (800m) north of Dryburgh. It was commissioned by the 11th Earl of Buchan and erected in 1814. The red sandstone statue was originally painted white. It can be accessed by a steep path from the B6356 or, more gently, from a car park to the north-east.

Wallace's Statue above Dryburgh has a view to the Eildon Hills (detour from walk)

Buckholm Tower (Walk 15)

Slightly harder walks of 2½ – 4 hours

walk 12

Whiteadder Valley and Edin's Hall Broch

Start: Abbey St Bathans

Distance: 5¼ miles (8.5km)

Height gain: 755 feet (230m)

Approximate time: 2¾ hours

Route terrain: Heath and field paths, lane and track

Parking: Car park by the Woodlands Café

OS maps: Landranger 67 (Duns, Dunbar & Eyemouth), Explorer 346 (Berwick-upon-Tweed)

GPS waypoints:
- NT 762 618
- Ⓐ NT 767 611
- Ⓑ NT 772 603
- Ⓒ NT 786 604
- Ⓓ NT 789 609
- Ⓔ NT 780 621

Few brochs exist outside the far north of Scotland and its islands – consequently Edin's Hall is something of an oddity. It is explored on this enjoyable walk along the valley of Whiteadder Water from Abbey St Bathans, returning by a pleasant country route to the north.

> **Abbey St Bathans** Despite the settlement's name, there never was an abbey. Rather, it was a small priory for Cistercian nuns, founded at the beginning of the 13th century by Ada, Countess of Dunbar. The place took its name from a 6th-century Irish monk from Iona, St Bathan, who supposedly founded a chapel here. The priory was destroyed by English troops in 1543 and its site has now been lost, although the small church, just up the road from the start of the walk, contains a funeral effigy of a prioress.

Follow the lane south to a wood yard, there leaving for a short stretch of riverside path on the left. Returning to the lane, carry on, gradually gaining height above the valley for ½ mile (800m). Where the lane bends sharply right, abandon it for a footpath signed to Edin's Hall Broch Ⓐ. Steps lead down beside the edge of Ellerburn Wood to a bridge. Turn briefly downstream before climbing over a shoulder to emerge from the trees. An obvious trod strikes across the open lower flank of Cockburn Law, gently rising above the Whiteadder Valley. After ½ mile (800m), approaching a stile, swing left down to a second stile, over which, climb to the broch Ⓑ.

Beyond the broch, the path falls across the hillside to a kissing-gate at the bottom end of a wall. Carry on at the edge of grazing above a steep wooded bank, crossing a couple of

The impressive remains of Edin's Hall Broch

Edin's Hall Broch

Occupying a commanding platform above a steep slope, the broch's structure is immediately apparent. Within the thickness of a massive drystone annular wall are several rooms and the remains of a staircase to a higher level. Originally it would have been at least two storeys high, the central area roofed over with timber beams. Built during the 1st century, it stands within an earlier extensive hillfort, whose double ditch and earth rampart defences are readily discernible. Later occupation of the site is revealed in several hut circles, some of which overlie the earlier structures and probably date to the Roman period during the 2nd century.

wall stiles before the path slants down to a lower pasture. Joining its left fence, continue above the river. In time, thorns squeeze the way to a gate, through which, the path drops to a track. Cross and continue behind a house to a bridge suspended above a rapid **C**, which impressively churns the peaty flow of Whiteadder Water after heavy rain.

A track winds away between the trees. Keep right to climb beside Otter Burn. Reaching a lane at the top **D** go left. Follow it uphill for a mile (1.6km), shortly leaving the woodland behind. Arriving at a junction **E**, go left to Blackerstone and The Retreat, but after ¼ mile (400m), where the lane then swings left, keep ahead on a broad track. It eventually meanders down to run at the edge of Butterwell Wood. Keep going for another ¼ mile (400m) before leaving over a redundant stile on the right. Signed to Abbey St Bathans, a clear path rises through the bracken and gorse of the hillside, before dropping into trees to meet a track bringing the Southern Upland Way from Cockburnspath to the river. Cross a bridge beside the ford to go back to the car park.

walk 13 Arnton Fell

Start
Second lay-by on right along unclassified lane, signed to Steele Road off B6399

Distance
5¼ miles (8.4km)

Height gain
1,115 feet (340m)

Approximate time
3 hours

Route terrain
Pathless moorland fell. Note: hillside closed between April 10 – May 1 during lambing

Parking
Limited roadside parking, do not obstruct passing place. Alternative roadside parking and walk start ½ mile (800m) further north (NY 511 941)

OS maps
Landranger 79 (Hawick & Eskdale), Explorer OL42 (Kielder Water & Forest)

GPS waypoints
- 🖉 NY 514 932
- Ⓐ NY 522 948
- Ⓑ NY 524 950
- Ⓒ NY 529 965
- Ⓓ NY 525 965
- Ⓔ NY 516 951

Arnton Fell is seemingly remote from anywhere, although until 40 years ago, the famous Waverley Line between Edinburgh and Carlisle ran below its eastern flank. The ascent of Arnton from the south and traverse of its broad, grassy ridge onto Blackwood Hill is rewarded by a superb view of Liddesdale and the hills that surround its head. Inexperienced walkers should choose a clear day.

🖉 A field gate opposite the lay-by gives access to the hillside. Strike half left past the end of a plantation, moving away to pick up a fence climbing on the right. Farther on, after passing a small plantation, carry on through a gate, steadily gaining height along the spur of the hill. Where the fence eventually curves right, break left, climbing more steeply to discover a triangulation pillar marking the end of the ridge Ⓐ. Isolated from the forest cloaking the eastern slope of the fell, it enjoys a magnificent panorama over the surrounding hills. To the west is Hermitage Castle, built in the 13th century to control one of the most fought-over valleys in the central borders. From here, it is much less forbidding than its reputation and perhaps suggests a visit later in the day.

With the strenuous part of the ascent now behind you, continue along the ridge towards a pair of gates. Through the left one, walk on past a pile of stones, which marks the first high point Ⓑ. A rough path runs on for a generous mile (1.6km) beside a plantation boundary, dipping gently before climbing to the somewhat higher summit of Blackwood Hill. Keep going beyond, descending to the corner of the fence Ⓒ.

Strike away, almost due west towards the distant castle. Descend steeply over rough ground to a grass track contouring the lower slopes of the hill Ⓓ. Follow it left for ½ mile (800m), ultimately fording a stream by Roughley Farm. Now gravel, the track continues along the valley for another ½ mile (800m) before fording Watt's Burn.

(If you are at the alternative parking, you may wish to continue with the track past Shaws to meet the lane by the bridge near Newlands.) Otherwise, as the track then curves away Ⓔ, branch left at a shallow angle, rising across the grassy hillside above the hollow of a small shale quarry. Carry on across the rough, pathless slope of the hill, eventually passing through an electric fence to skirt the top of a small conifer

plantation, Shaws Brae. Maintain the same direction to the corner of a second enclosure, now regenerating after felling.

Again cross an electric strand and briefly follow a fence on the right. When that turns down, keep ahead, later passing above more plantation. Cross a gate there and bear right to negotiate the deep ditch of Paddington Sike. Walk on paralleling the Steele Plantation on your right, eventually picking up your outward steps at its far end to return to the lane. •

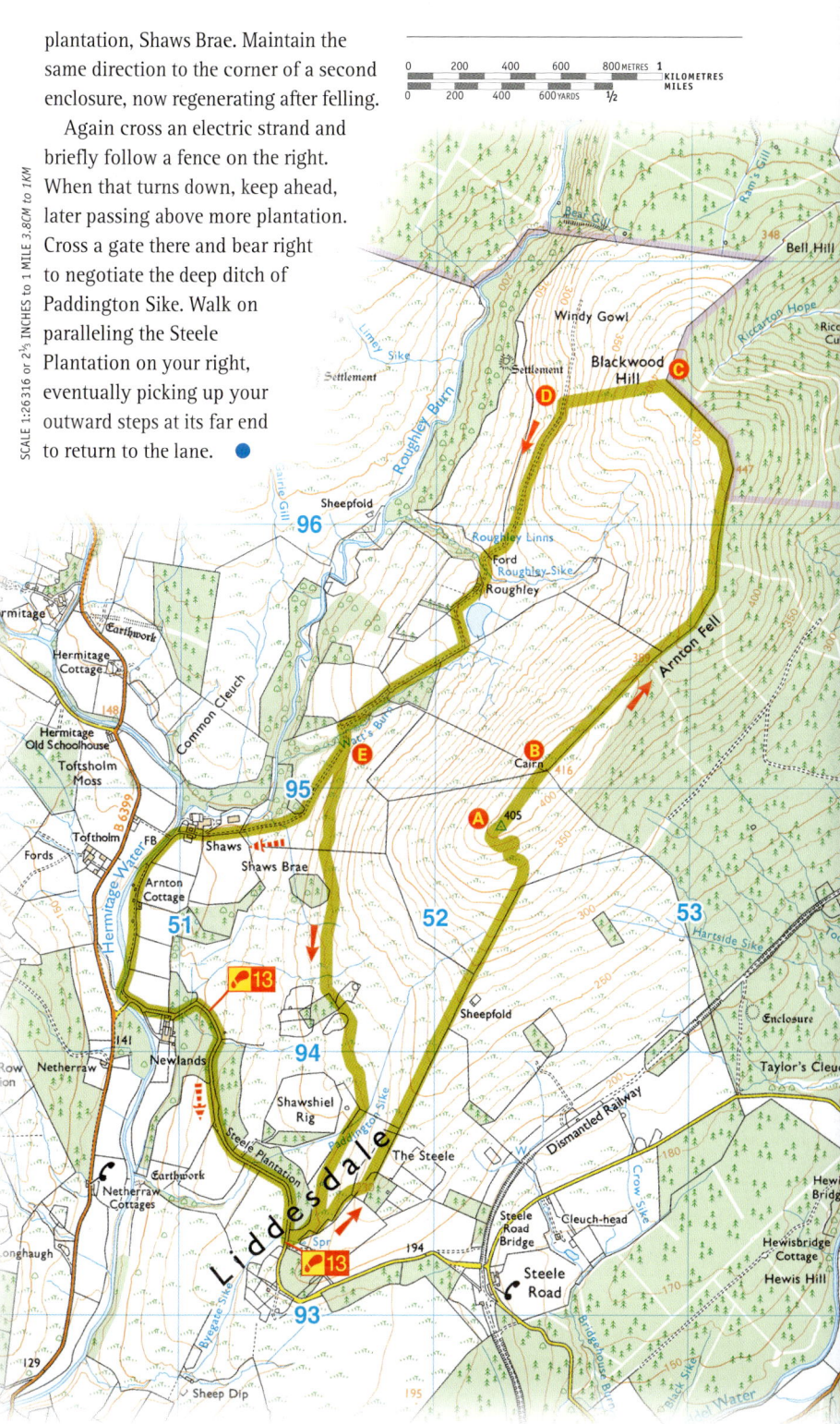

ARNTON FELL • 39

walk 14

Melrose and the Eildon Hills

Start: Melrose

Distance: 5¼ miles (8.4km)

Height gain: 1,475 feet (450m)

Approximate time: 3 hours

Route terrain: Generally good, but occasionally steep paths

Parking: Melrose

OS maps: Landranger 73 (Peebles, Galashiels & Selkirk), Explorer 338 (Galashiels, Selkirk & Melrose)

GPS waypoints:
- 🏁 NT 547 339
- Ⓐ NT 547 337
- Ⓑ NT 550 325
- Ⓒ NT 548 322
- Ⓓ NT 554 328
- Ⓔ NT 563 336
- Ⓕ NT 561 341

The striking landmarks of the three peaks of the Eildon Hills all offer stunning views from their summits. This walk takes in the two highest, returning in a roundabout route beside the River Tweed. Although fairly short, the climb onto middle peak is quite steep, as is the descent from northern hill.

🏁 Begin from the Market Cross in the Square, leaving south along Dingleton Road, which climbs away beneath the bypass. Some 100 yards beyond the bridge, look for a stepped path signed as the Eildon Walk and St Cuthbert's Way Ⓐ, which drops between the terraces to a bridge over Malthouse Burn.

The onward path rises left behind the cottages before turning up a long flight of steps beside a wood. Over a stile, the way continues energetically upwards, offering an excuse to pause and admire the retrospective view over the town and its abbey. Through a couple of gates, cross the end of a track and resume the steep ascent. Emerging through a gate onto the open hillside, walk up to a three-way signpost and go right. A short level stretch leads to another junction. There turn left, resuming the climb to a shallow saddle between the northern and middle hills Ⓑ, where a superb view suddenly opens to the south.

Tackle Mid Hill first, taking the path off right. Keep ahead over a crossing path and then ignore successive paths branching off first right and then left to begin the steep ascent

Melrose Abbey

40 ● WALK 14

of the hill's northern flank. Higher up, the gradient briefly eases before the path swings left in a final determined attack of the summit cone **C**. The panorama from the top is quite magnificent, a topograph helping you to identify the surrounding hills. On a shelf, just below to the right is a burial cairn, while to the south is the lowest hill of the group.

Return to the saddle **B** and continue ahead onto the northern hill. The climb is less strenuous and although all upward paths will take you to the top,

Melrose Abbey

Aidan, the Ionian missionary who brought Christianity to Northumbria, founded the first monastery at Melrose in AD 660. Cuthbert began his vocation here and became its second prior, and Melrose is traditionally one of the places where the Lindisfarne monks laid his body during their wandering search for a new home. The present ruins are of a Cistercian foundation under David I in 1131, the town growing to serve both the needs of the monks and pilgrims visiting the abbey church. Like other border towns, Melrose periodically suffered from the attacks and reprisals of both sides, the abbey finally being destroyed around 1550. Sir Walter Scott and the Duke of Buccleuch were responsible for its restoration in 1822.

MELROSE AND THE EILDON HILLS • 41

the broadest trail takes the easiest line to a low pile of stones marking the summit ⓓ.

Carry on along a short grassy ridge, at the end of which bear left on a path descending through the heather and blaeberry. The way progressively steepens to a waymark. Bear left, continuing straight down the hill between patches of gorse. Meeting a junction of paths before a line of beech masking a plantation of pine, go left, shortly passing through a gate. An old hedged path runs down to meet a lane, formerly the main road into the town.

Go right, passing through a barrier to find a stone stele 100 yards farther on. 'This stone marks the site of the Eildon Tree, where legend says Thomas the Rhymer met the Queen of the Fairies and here he was inspired to utter the first notes of the Scottish Muse'. The original site lay somewhat to the south, but the stone was relocated in 1970.

Return through the barrier and take the track just beyond on the right ⓔ, which falls between the fields. Swing left at the bottom and then leave through a gate on the right to reach the main A6091. Cross using the underpass on the right. Emerging beyond, keep ahead beneath an old railway bridge to a T-junction of tracks ⓕ.

Go right to a cottage and then turn left down Claymires Lane. Coming out onto a street at the bottom walk right and then almost immediately left into Eddy Road. It soon degrades to a rough track, from the end of which a trod continues over a footbridge to the Tweed.

Turn upstream, shortly passing along a walkway to carry on by the river at the edge of a large grazing meadow. Reaching the far side, the route climbs over the end of a sturdy stone wall known as Battery Dyke. It runs above the river for ¼ mile (400m) and used to carry the path along its top. However, the way now winds through the trees beside it, continuing beyond its end past a waste-water treatment plant and rugby ground. The path eventually leads into the corner of a small field. Go left at the edge to emerge onto a lane. Turn left again past the rugby ground to a junction. Go right to pass the abbey and Priorwood Garden and keep ahead back to the centre of Melrose. ●

Melrose town centre and market cross

Buckholm Circular, Galashiels

walk 15

Start	Galashiels
Distance	5½ miles (8.7km)
Height gain	740 feet (225m)
Approximate time	3 hours
Route terrain	Woodland paths; grassy field paths and tracks, prone to being muddy in places
Parking	Ladhope car park, Halliburton, Galashiels
OS maps	Landranger 73 (Peebles, Galashiels & Selkirk), Explorer 338 (Galashiels, Selkirk & Melrose)

GPS waypoints

- NT 489 367
- Ⓐ NT 492 368
- Ⓑ NT 495 372
- Ⓒ NT 483 378
- Ⓓ NT 484 386
- Ⓔ NT 497 393
- Ⓕ NT 496 387

This circumnavigation of Buckholm Hill offers views in all directions. As you pass through open wood pasture, 100 feet (30m) above the busy town of Galashiels, it feels as if you are entering another world. Silence reigns as you walk round the back of the hill through rolling farmland. Two landmarks encountered on this walk, Buckholm Tower and Dobies Grave, have tragic legends associated with them.

Yellow arrows mark the Buckholm Circular, which is followed until Ⓔ where our route returns by the Dobies Grave path. The tracks are muddy in a few wet places, so boots are recommended.

Ruined farm and tower at Old Buckholm

Walk out of the top of Ladhope car park and up the pavement for 100 yards. Where the road bends right, bear left on a path by a fingerpost, signed Ladhope Glen and Buckholm Circular. Soon fork right to walk up the left side of the stream valley. Climb some steps as you ascend and emerge onto a road by a fingerpost at the bottom of Heatheryett Cemetery car park Ⓐ (an alternative start point).

Turn right, signed Buckholm Circular, and continue at the top of the car park on a track marked with a yellow arrow. Keep ahead when a path branches into trees opposite a field gate. At a high metal fence, bear left to a kissing-gate beside a field gate. Continue up the left side of a field of close-cropped grass. In about 100 yards, pass the bottom end of the Dobies Grave path at a fingerpost Ⓑ.

BUCKHOLM CIRCULAR, GALASHIELS • 43

Dobies Grave is marked by a large cairn

Continue uphill beside the fence and turn left at the top corner. Follow the fence, which kinks slightly left and goes a little downhill. Go through a gate in a wall into an area of wood pasture planted by the Borders Forest Trust, passing a bench overlooking Galashiels. Cattle graze here and the trees are protected by fences. The grassy track, now more definite, stays on the level while the field boundary gradually trends downhill.

Soon, go through a gate in another stone wall and keep ahead on the level across pasture, picking up a slight sheep trod and (looking at the map) staying just above the 200m contour. A further gate leads to more wood pasture. A fence rises up from the left and you continue above it on a more definite track. After passing through banks of gorse it curves right into a valley and runs uphill beside a wall. Beyond a gate, Buckholm Tower lies ahead beside a small farmhouse **C**.

Before the ruined buildings, enclosed by a fence with a Keep Out sign, angle right on the track. It climbs above the buildings then dips down to run alongside a stone wall with a fine view of the valley to the left. Beyond a cattle grid and gate the track runs down towards Buckholm Cottages. Meet a minor road opposite the cottages **D**.

Turn right and walk up the road for 1 mile (1.6km). Eventually it begins going downhill and, just after a small shed in the field on the left, turn right down a track towards a corner of forest. By a small parking area, before the gate into the forest, leave the Buckholm Circular and go right into a field by the gate or over the stile beside it **E**.

Walk up the pasture field, gradually bearing right towards the skyline. Ascend a gully to the large, solitary cairn marking Dobies Grave, just below a corner of wall and fence. Don't be misled by the more extensive piles of stones in the middle of the field, which appear to be the remains of buildings. Keep on over the brow of the hill to a stile and gate in the wall ahead **F**.

> **Buckholm Tower** This rectangular tower house, built in 1582, is believed by locals to be haunted. A former laird, James Pringle, was a violent man who terrorised women. He helped dragoons capture two Covenanters, who were left overnight in his dungeon for safe keeping. After an evening spent drinking heavily, he beat the men to death and hung them on meat hooks. Ghosts may be seen around the ruins.

Cross over and keep ahead on a more visible path. Beyond another gate and stile in a fence, the path comes close to the forest. After a ford across a stream, it runs beside a wall then crosses another wall by a gate and ladder stile. Now the indented path curves round the hillside ahead. On arriving back at the fingerpost at B, turn left and retrace your steps through the gate and back down past the cemetery to return to the start.

Dobies Grave This large cairn supposedly marks the spot where a piper called Dobie failed to win a wager. According to legend, he accepted a bet that he could play the bagpipes all the way from Lauder to Galashiels. On this final climb, before his destination came into sight, he collapsed and died.

0 200 400 600 800 METRES 1 KILOMETRES

0 200 400 600 YARDS ½ MILES

SCALE 1:25 000 or 2½ INCHES to 1 MILE *4CM to 1KM*

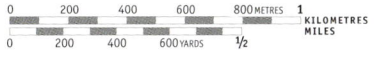

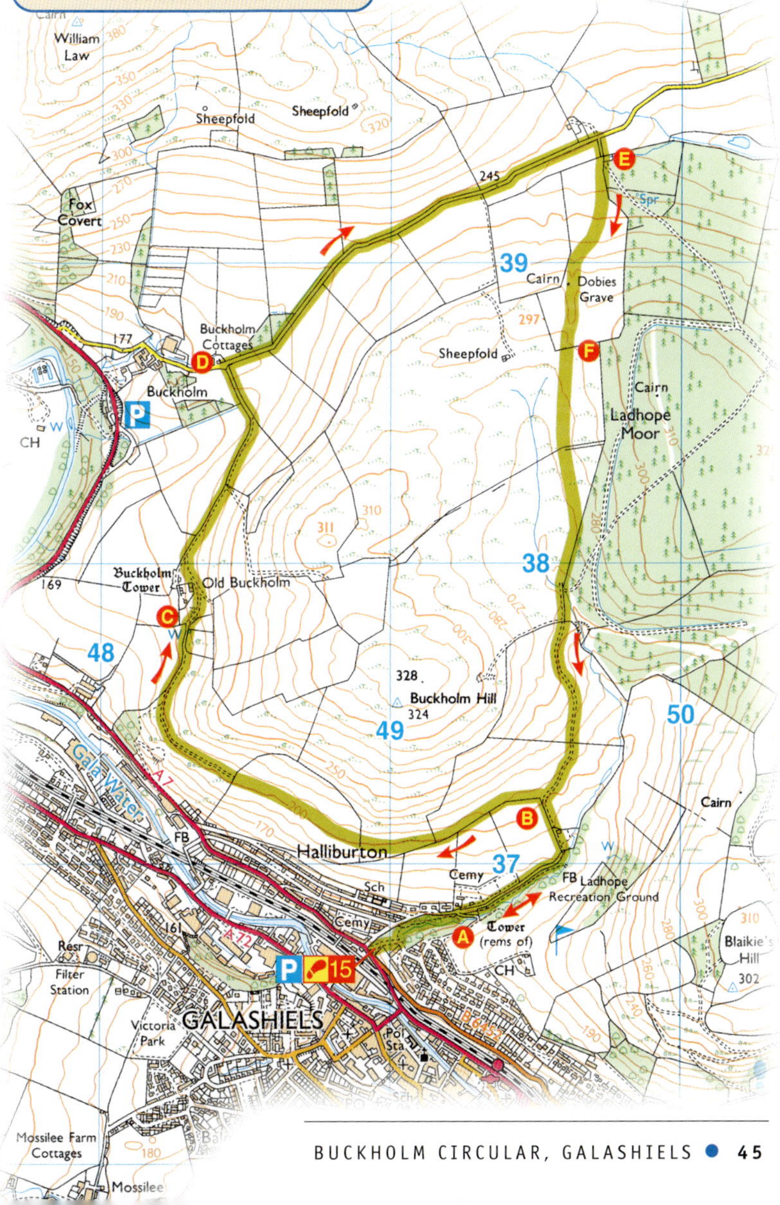

walk 16

Coldingham Bay and St Abb's Head

Start
Coldingham Bay, ¾ mile (1.2km) east of Coldingham village

Distance
5¾ miles (9.1km)

Height gain
935 feet (285m)

Approximate time
3 hours

Route terrain
Clear paths and tracks, cliff edge

Parking
Car park at start

OS maps
Landranger 67 (Duns, Dunbar & Eyemouth), Explorer 346 (Berwick-upon-Tweed)

GPS waypoints
- NT 915 665
- Ⓐ NT 919 672
- Ⓑ NT 916 674
- Ⓒ NT 913 691
- Ⓓ NT 908 689
- Ⓔ NT 913 685
- Ⓕ NT 912 673
- Ⓖ NT 913 667

St Abb's Head is one of the spectacular sections of the eastern coastline, a progression of high sandstone cliffs twisting back from tiny coves and towering stacks. The popular beach at Coldingham and the headland nature reserve are both visited on this grand ramble above the cliffs, which returns via an inland loch and ancient path.

> **St Abbs** St Abbs takes its name from Æbbe, daughter of the Northumbrian king, Æthefrith, who founded a monastery following shipwreck in a storm upon this treacherous coast. The settlement was subsequently destroyed by an accidental fire, supposedly in retribution for 'disorderly' behaviour between the monks and nuns. The 12th-century priory at Coldingham was a Benedictine house for monks and suffered fluctuating fortunes until the Scottish Reformation in 1560 put a stop to monasticism. The church continued in use by the parish, although was badly damaged when Cromwell passed by in 1650.

Turn right out of the car park and keep ahead to the beach, where, in the best seaside tradition, there is a motley line of bathing huts. Turn left along the head of the beach towards a gnarled stack rising above the rocks at the far end of the shore. However, before that point, a flight of steps takes the route up to join a tarmac path along the clifftop to St Abbs. Reaching a signpost, turn left along a street lined by low cottages, Murrayfield.

Go right at the T-junction Ⓐ and then swing left with the main street as it curves high above the harbour. Keep left again at the far end, passing the church where you can abandon the tarmac for a parallel footpath on the left. When it finishes, cross to a path opposite Ⓑ, which is signed to St Abb's Head and runs away beside a high stone wall.

Regaining the coast, climb above Starney Bay and past a succession of inaccessible coves and sea-washed rocks before dropping to the head of Horsecastle Bay. Turning from the sea, follow the foot of Kirk Hill, part of which is a protected habitat for the northern brown argus butterfly.

Beyond, the path gains height towards the coast, giving sight of the sea once more. The lighthouse also comes into view, set upon a squat building partway down a spit in order to shine below the fog that often obscures the clifftops. Pass left of the lighthouse cottages and drop to a metalled drive **C**. However, first you might climb left to a hilltop viewpoint for a magnificent panorama that sweeps inland across the Cheviot and border hills.

Instead of simply following the lane, take a convoluted path above the dramatic cliffs, but *be wary of the precipice*.

The path winds back to join the lane as it drops steeply through a hairpin to the head of a small bay. Climb away, but leave just before a cattle grid **D**, following a path through a gate in an intervening fence and past a reedbed at the head of Mire Loch. The way weaves through scrub above the western bank, meeting a track at the far end **E**. Head uphill to rejoin the lighthouse lane, which wanders on for some ¾ mile (1.2km) to Northfield Farm.

Approaching the main lane, turn back left **F** to a car park, taking a path at the far side past the information centre and **seasonal café**. Carry on along the road, which as before can be avoided by parallel paths on the left and then the right. Retrace your steps above the harbour, turning right into Creel Road. This time, however, keep ahead to the end of the street and continue along a contained path. An ancient way, it was used by Coldingham's monks and fishermen to reach their boats moored below St Abbs. Becoming hedged, the path falls into a dip **G**, where a path is signed left to Coldingham Sands. Reaching a lane, turn right back to the start.

Seabirds

Thousands of seabirds nest here in late spring; guillemots and razorbills crowding narrow ledges on the stacks, while kittiwakes and fulmars build nests on the sheer cliff. A handful of puffins hide their eggs in tiny crevices, while on the slabs below you will see shags and herring gulls.

walk 17

Selkirk Hill, Whitmuirhill Loch and Lindean Loch

Start
Selkirk Hill

Distance
5¾ miles (9.25km)

Height gain
710 feet (215m)

Approximate time
3 hours

Route terrain
Grass and earth paths over open hillside and around lochs, plus short sections of road

Parking
Selkirk Hill car park, on A699 1 mile (1.6km) east of Selkirk

OS maps
Landranger 73 (Peebles, Galashiels & Selkirk), Explorer 338 (Galashiels, Selkirk & Melrose)

GPS waypoints
- NT 483 281
- Ⓐ NT 480 277
- Ⓑ NT 489 275
- Ⓒ NT 494 271
- Ⓓ NT 501 277
- Ⓔ NT 498 285
- Ⓕ NT 497 296
- Ⓖ NT 489 293
- Ⓗ NT 486 286

A wonderful view over Selkirk is gained early on in this walk, which starts on the hill above the town. The route then circuits high, rolling countryside with distant prospects to all points of the compass. It passes Selkirk Racecourse, which claims to be the oldest in the world. Hollows in the hills contain two lochs, with lots of birdlife. The second, Lindean Loch, is a nature reserve and has a path running all the way round it.

The route is marked by posts with Selkirk Paths disks and yellow arrows indicating the direction.

With your back to the road, climb steps at the left end of the car park to a fence. Turn right and, without crossing it at a stile or later wooden gate, walk to the top of Selkirk Hill, where a viewpoint indicator and bench overlook Selkirk. Continue ahead, downhill to a metal gate and stile in a wall Ⓐ, and turn hard left here.

Walk along an old trackway that runs along the lower edge of a line of mature beech trees. Where they end, keep ahead via a gate and stile, with a wall on your left. When you reach a broader woodland strip, go through a gate in the wall and continue in the same direction on a track up the left side of the trees. At the top (987 feet/301m) Ⓑ, go right through field gates then turn left beside the rightmost of two diverging walls towards the white railings of the former racecourse.

Selkirk Racecourse on Gala Rig

Follow the curving wall outside the racecourse then go through a field gate at its south-west corner. Continue downhill with a wall on your right (or walk through the racecourse if you want to remain on higher ground). After descending a steeper slope between gorse bushes, bear left on a grassy path. At the bottom **C** turn left before two wooden gates, following a path through bracken.

> **Selkirk Racecourse** Gala Rig is claimed to be the location of the oldest racecourse still in use. Selkirk town records first document racing in 1715, but it is believed to have started in the mid-17th century. The last official meet of the Racing Calendar was held in 1881, but the course is now used by the Selkirk Flapping Association for horse races that are run outside Jockey Club rules.

SCALE 1:25,000 or 2½ INCHES to 1 MILE 4CM to 1KM

SELKIRK HILL, WHITMUIRHILL LOCH AND LINDEAN LOCH

Stay above a strip of mixed woodland bordering Whitmuirhill Loch, which is vegetated at its west end. Meet scrubby hawthorn and keep above a fence and later a wall round woodland. When the wall swings left, follow it uphill to arrive at the east end of the racecourse. Cross the wall here by gate or stile and walk along a grassy track beside conifers to another gate and stile. Keep ahead across a field to a kissing-gate and turn left onto a minor road **D**.

Walk down a beech avenue then turn right along the A699 for 100 yards before crossing over. *This is a fast road so take care and step onto the verge if you hear traffic.* Walk down a path with a tree-lined fence on the right and young conifers on the left. Then bear slightly right between fences under mature beech trees. Keep ahead through two wooden gates, now with a wall on the left. In the dip, a stream flows under the path into Murder Moss. Continue to a gate in the wall **E** where the Iron Age fort (worth a detour) rises on the left.

Here the path swings right beside a ruined wall. After 200 yards, turn left through a gate in a wall and walk beside it to a gate into Lindean Loch Nature Reserve. Turn left on a path that arcs round the west end of the water. On the far side, turn left by a post with a yellow arrow and through a gate. Walk up the edge of a field containing a tall TV mast. Follow the wall to a gate onto a minor road **F** and turn left, now on the Borders Abbeys Way.

At Shawmount, where there are buildings either side, go through a gate on the left and along a path fenced beside the road, signed for Selkirk Hill. Enter a field by a gate and keep ahead to the corner then go through another gate and left, as indicated by a Borders Abbeys Way arrow. At metal gates join a track **G** and turn right along it.

Curve round the hillside, going through three gates to reach a stone bridge over Dean Burn. Immediately beyond, go through a kissing-gate on the left, leaving the Borders Abbeys Way. In a few paces turn left by a post with a yellow arrow – these mark the rest of the route. Soon cross the stream by a footbridge. At a junction by a post **H** turn right, as indicated.

Beyond a plank bridge, keep left. Cross a footbridge over the outflow channel then another plank bridge, and keep ahead to skirt the pond. Fork left and at the west end of the pond turn left past a wooden shed then left again beside a fence. Keep uphill to a wall and turn right through a kissing-gate onto the golf course. Walk along the left edge, climbing beside the wall to the top corner. Nearing the road, go right as signed and emerge onto the A699 via a golf course path opposite the car park. *Cross with care as there is poor visibility on the bend.*

North from the Borders Abbeys Way

Peebles and the River Tweed

Hardly anywhere along the length of the River Tweed is its course less than attractive, but the stretch above the ancient border town of Peebles is particularly fine. This circuit begins along the northern bank below the striking Neidpath Castle, generally following the course of an old railway to Lyne Bridge. There is a flavour of the surrounding countryside too, as the route climbs to the superb viewpoint at Manor Sware on its meandering return to the town.

walk 18

Start
Peebles

Distance
7¼ miles (11.8km)

Height gain
490 feet (150m)

Approximate time
3½ hours

Route terrain
Clear paths and tracks

Parking
Swimming Pool car park (Pay and Display)

OS maps
Landranger 73 (Peebles, Galashiels & Selkirk), Explorer 337 (Peebles & Innerleithen)

GPS waypoints
- NT 249 403
- Ⓐ NT 232 401
- Ⓑ NT 228 395
- Ⓒ NT 209 399
- Ⓓ NT 206 397
- Ⓔ NT 217 388
- Ⓕ NT 230 393
- Ⓖ NT 244 401

Peebles
A favourite residence of the kings of Scotland, Peebles was a royal burgh by the time of King David I. Although escaping much of the border conflict, it was razed by the British in 1549 and suffered again a century later when occupied by Cromwell's troops. Despite poverty during the 18th century, the railway age brought better times and it gained a reputation as a fashionable spa with the opening of the Peebles Hydro in 1881. An attractive town, it has no shortage of fine eating places and is a popular centre for walkers, anglers and golfers. One of the high spots of its calendar is the Beltane Festival, a colourful week of events held each June that has its origins in a Celtic celebration marking the return of the summer.

Leave the far end of the Swimming Pool car park along a riverside path, crossing a bridge spanning Eddlestone Water. Walk on by the river, later turning up steps. At the top, go left behind Hay Lodge Hospital, dropping beyond to Hay Lodge Park. Passing a footbridge, continue through the park, beyond which a more rugged path winds into a narrowing valley.

The valley sides once more draw in, forcing the onward path into undulations along the steep wooded bank. Pretty views open through the trees, which soon stand back to reveal the Neidpath Viaduct. It carried a picturesque branch line between

Neidpath Castle
Overlooking a clearing, Neidpath Castle was built in the 14th century by Sir William Hay, the Sheriff of Peebles, on the site of an earlier castle. After changing allegiances, his descendant John Hay sided with the Royalists and, according to some, the castle surrendered only after a damaging siege by Cromwell's forces. Although later modernised, the castle fell into neglect and the romantic ruin inspired Sir Walter Scott to pen a poem about its ghost, *The Maid of Neidpath*.

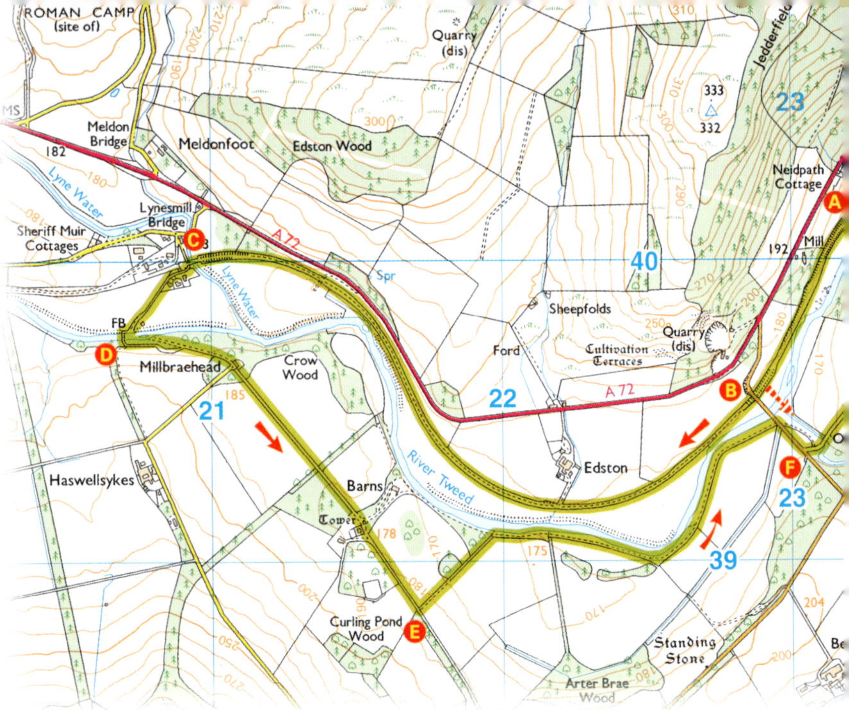

Symington and Peebles, which opened in 1860. After crossing the viaduct, the line disappeared into a tunnel for the final stretch into Peebles.

Through a gate beneath the bridge Ⓐ, mount the embankment and walk away along the trackbed. Emerging from a gentle curve the line runs dead straight above riverside meadows, the trees thinning to give a memorable view to the hills. After ½ mile (800m), a missing bridge forces you off the embankment to cross a lane Ⓑ. *To the left, Manor Bridge offers a shortcut to the return route.* The main route, however, climbs back onto the embankment opposite, following it for 1½ miles (2.4km) to a bridge over Lyne Water Ⓒ. Drop to the narrow lane below and go right. Soon degrading to a track, it leads to a footbridge across the River Tweed Ⓓ.

The path swings downstream along a woodland strip above the river, before long joining a broader path that leads to

Lynesmill Bridge

0	200	400	600	800 METRES	1 KILOMETRES
0	200	400	600 YARDS	½	MILES

SCALE 1:25 000 or 2½ INCHES to 1 MILE 4CM to 1KM

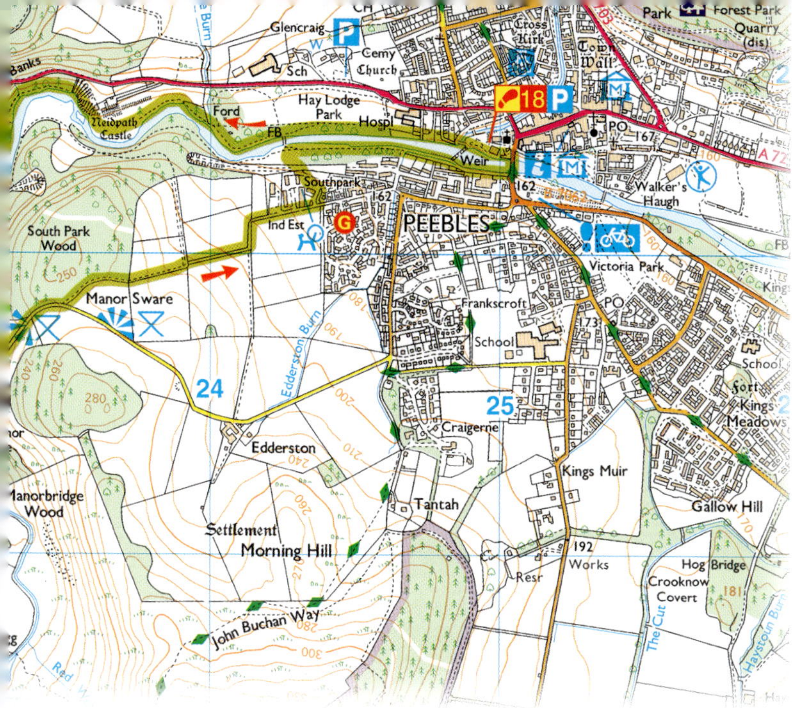

a cottage at Millbraehead. Keep ahead along a private track onto the Wemyss and March Estate. Signed as the Tweed Walk, it is a lovely avenue of stately old lime trees, which runs dead-straight between the fields and eventually leads to a junction overlooked by a 15th-century tower house, Barns Tower. Again go forward, passing the stables and as you continue along the track, look back left to see the later mansion, built in the 18th century once peace had settled on the troubled border.

After another ¼ mile (400m), the Tweed Walk is directed off over a stile on the left **E**. A green track across the fields takes you back to the riverbank. Continue downstream beside the meadows on a tree-lined path to Manor Bridge.

Join the lane and walk away from the bridge, soon bearing left at a fork **F** down to Old Manor Bridge, a graceful, single arch of stone built in 1702. Beyond, a narrow lane, now closed to traffic, rises steadily uphill, passing a viewpoint towards the top from which there is a stunning retrospective vista along the valley.

Carry on around the bend to find a gate on the left into South Park Wood, from which a path is signed to Peebles. Where it then divides, branch right within the fringe of the wood. Reaching the corner, leave over a stile and head down at the perimeter of grazing. A view opens to the town below, the towers and steeples of its churches standing prominent above the other buildings. From a gate at the bottom corner, a broad, fenced path winds down, emerging in South Parks on the outskirts of Peebles. Walk on between housing and a small industrial estate. Just past South Park Garage **G**, turn off left and wind down between small units. Continue along a track through woodland to come out on the riverbank. Turn right along the waterside path back to the town. Climb out to the main road and turn over the bridge to return to the swimming baths and car park. ●

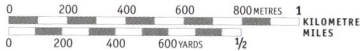

walk 19

Kelso, Roxburgh and the River Teviot

Start
Kelso Town Hall

Distance
7½ miles (12.1km)

Height gain
360 feet (110m)

Approximate time
3½ hours

Route terrain
Clear paths. Note: the riverside return may be flooded following exceptional rain

Parking
Kelso

OS maps
Landranger 74 (Kelso & Coldstream), Explorer 339 (Kelso, Coldstream & Lower Tweed Valley)

GPS waypoints
- NT 727 339
- Ⓐ NT 727 335
- Ⓑ NT 723 327
- Ⓒ NT 703 304
- Ⓓ NT 697 305
- Ⓔ NT 703 313
- Ⓕ NT 719 336

Exploring the Teviot Valley upstream of its confluence with the River Tweed, this walk begins from the ancient abbey town of Kelso. It follows the course of a disused railway to an impressive viaduct above the present day village of Roxburgh before returning along the riverbank past the once-grand castle upon which the historical royal burgh of Roxburgh was centred.

Kelso Abbey

Kelso grew around the abbey, founded by King David I in 1128. Despite centuries of border raids, it became the wealthiest monastery in Scotland until the English largely destroyed its fabric in 1547. Following the Reformation in 1560, it fell derelict, much of its stone being pillaged for reuse in the town's buildings.

With your back to the town hall, cross the impressive cobbled square and turn left into Bridge Street. Walk past the abbey ruins and over the Tweed on John Rennie's elegant bridge before dropping left into the park Ⓐ. Steps at the far corner regain the road beside the Millenium Viewpoint, which you should follow uphill. Swing sharp right at the junction along Jedburgh Road, soon leaving the town's houses behind.

Approaching the main road, cross to the entrance of Wallacenick Farm where there is a rough track off to the left Ⓑ, the course of the old railway. After ¼ mile (400m), watch for a waymarked path forking off left, which winds beside a fence into

54 • WALK 19

a field. Follow the edge right, turning the corner to a small gate. Go right and left within the fringe of a small wood, leaving through a gate at the far corner. Bear left, climbing past the abutment of a bridge to rejoin the trackbed. The way meanders pleasantly along the hillside, affording a fine panorama across the valley. To the north, beyond the ruin of Roxburgh Castle is Floors Castle, while out west are the distinctive summits of the Eildon Hills.

Farther along, the track becomes

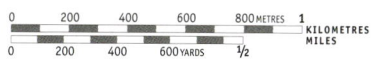

SCALE 1:25 000 or 2½ INCHES to 1 MILE 4CM to 1KM

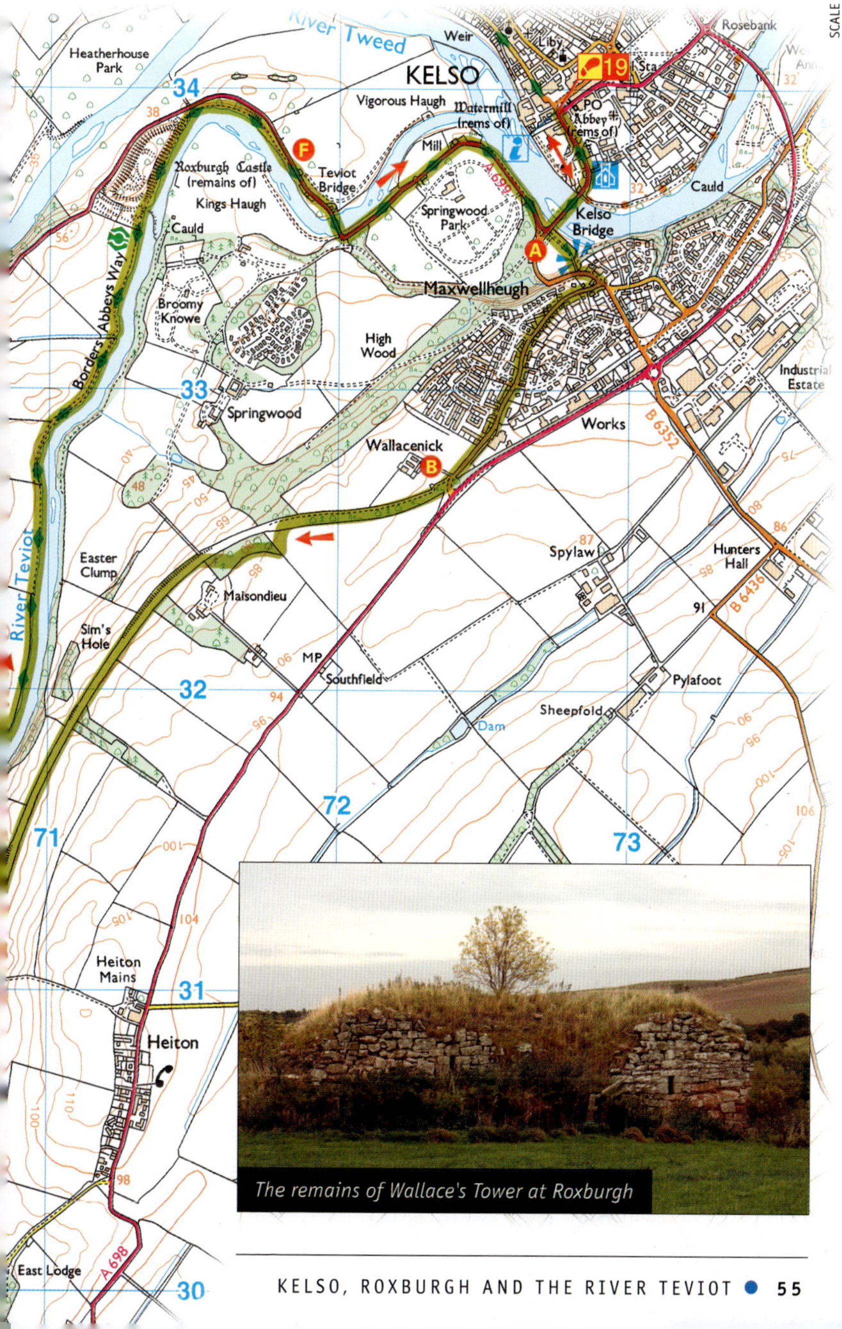

The remains of Wallace's Tower at Roxburgh

> **Roxburgh**
>
> The ancient royal burgh of Roxburgh lay within the protection of the castle on the spit of high land between the Teviot and Tweed rivers. It was taken several times by the English, in whose hands it remained from 1334 until 1460, when the castle was finally retaken by the Scots and demolished.

increasingly wooded, eventually curving towards the Roxburgh Viaduct. Although the route drops right at a waymark just before the viaduct **C**, it is worth continuing onto the bridge for the view. Return to the descending path, which leads to a narrow lane. At the foot of the viaduct, go right to find a footbridge, piggybacking the cutwaters across the river.

Following a sign for Lovers' Lane, cross ahead, but immediately bear right onto a contained path rising beside the embankment. At the top, there is a glimpse back through the hedge to Wallace's Tower, the remains of a 16th-century tower house. The path ends at a junction beside the demolished bridges of Roxburgh Junction **D**.

Turn right through the village and carry on past Roxburgh Mill, where the lane briefly runs beside the river. As the lane bends away, leave over the second of two stiles on the right waymarked the Borders Abbeys Way **E**. Follow the field boundary right and then round the corner to continue above a low cliff overlooking the river, dropping at the end of the second field to a riverside path. *Exceptionally, the river may flood its bank, in which case you must either retrace your route or follow the road back to Kelso.*

After a goodly mile (1.6km), the path passes beneath the ruins of Roxburgh Castle, which can be accessed over a stile.

Beyond, the river curves sharply right, a flight of steps soon lifting the path from the bank. After passing behind a cottage, walk out to the main road **F** and follow it right over Teviot Bridge. Carry on to pass the confluence of the two rivers and turn back into Kelso. ●

Kelso's five-arched bridge, designed by John Rennie in 1803

Denholm Dean and Bedrule

walk 20

Start
Denholm

Distance
7¼ miles (11.6km)

Height gain
1,050 feet (320m)

Approximate time
3¾ hours

Route terrain
Grassy paths; field and woodland tracks; minor roads

Parking
Parking around Denholm Green

OS maps
Landranger 79 (Hawick & Eskdale), Explorer 331 (Teviotdale South)

GPS waypoints
- NT 568 184
- Ⓐ NT 572 181
- Ⓑ NT 580 180
- Ⓒ NT 588 172
- Ⓓ NT 597 177
- Ⓔ NT 599 179
- Ⓕ NT 587 183
- Ⓖ NT 573 174
- Ⓗ NT 567 178

Situated in a beautiful part of Teviotdale, Denholm is a delightful start point for this figure-of-eight route. The walk follows the well-marked Borders Abbeys Way to the ancient hamlet of Bedrule, which takes its name from Rule Water, Gaelic for 'the roaring stream'. It returns through Denholm Dean, which now feels quite wild, although in the 19th century it was a woodland pleasure garden with a tea pavilion.

> **Denholm** When Denholm was laid out as a planned village around the Green in the 17th century, stone buildings replaced the original hamlet that had been burnt in repeated border raids. The Green was used for holding markets and grazing livestock. The impressive spire of Leyden's Monument stands at its centre. It was erected in 1861, to commemorate the life of Dr John Leyden, an antiquarian, physician and poet. The thatched cottage he was born in is to the north of the Green. On the south side, look out for the unusual Text House. The white, three-storey structure was erected by Dr John Haddon, a local philanthropist.

The walk can be shortened by 1¼ miles (2km) by omitting the section from Ⓓ to Ⓔ.

From the south-east corner of the Green, head east along Main Street and Eastgate towards Kelso. Turn first right up The Loaning and keep straight ahead when the road becomes a track, passing a fingerpost for the Borders Abbeys Way. Climb uphill and turn left at the top of the first field, where there is a view back over the village Ⓐ.

The track curves uphill between lush hedgerows. Beyond a kissing-gate keep ahead, enjoying views north and east. At the top, go through two gates to an open field and turn left along the field edge. At a fingerpost Ⓑ, turn right along the top of the next field, still on the Borders Abbeys Way.

Beyond a gate, descend past a barn and through another gate with a stile to cross a bridge at Spital Tower. Turn right in front of a house and follow the track past another gate and stile into pasture. Where the stony track bends hard right, keep straight ahead on grass – as indicated by a post with an arrow – towards a gate in a wall. Go through and keep straight ahead (there is one post on the top of the rise in the field) to another gate in a stone wall Ⓒ.

Once over, walk left down the field edge and, as you near a

Bedrule church

> **Bedrule Church** Early medieval carved stones have been found on this ancient religious site, which pilgrims visited on their way to Melrose Abbey. Bedrule Castle was built nearby in the 13th century and became the seat of Clan Turnbull in the 15th century. The village was the birthplace of Bishop Turnbull, who founded Glasgow University in 1451. The present church dates from 1804, but has been reshaped twice. Its stained glass windows, which depict stylised military scenes, are a memorial to those who died in the Great War (1914–18).

the village hall, turn left on a road past a row of white cottages to Bedrule Church **E**. A mound to the north-west of the church was the site of Bedrule Castle.

Return the same way to **D** then keep

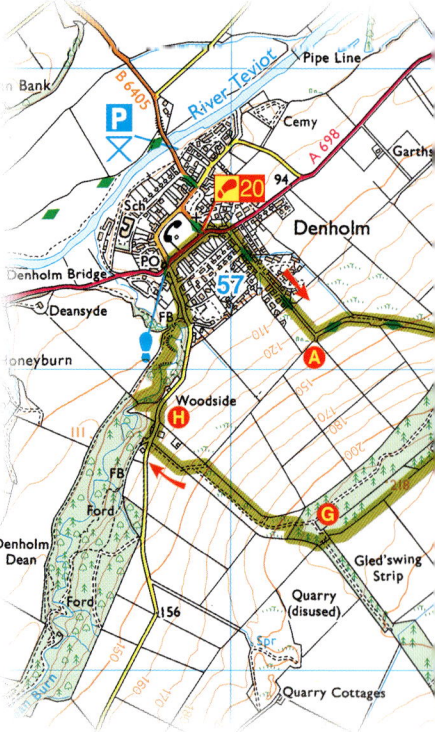

wood, bear right to walk along its edge. Go over a stile by a gate in a fence and curve left to another stile into the wood. Keep ahead on a track through the trees and turn right at a post. The track leaves the wood, becomes grassy and runs downhill to a road. Follow the road ahead, downhill to a T-junction **D**.

Turn right (or left to omit Bedrule) and cross a stone bridge. Rise up to a T-junction by a war memorial and go left, staying on the road when the Borders Abbeys Way branches right. By

58 ● WALK 20

Fields rising to the south near Towerburn

ahead along the road towards Denholm. In just over ¾ mile (1.2km), turn sharp left up a minor road signed Towerburn and Spital Tower. At a fingerpost, turn right through a gate on the path to Denholm and walk ahead beside a fence. At the end of the field go over a

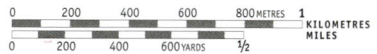

DENHOLM DEAN AND BEDRULE • 59

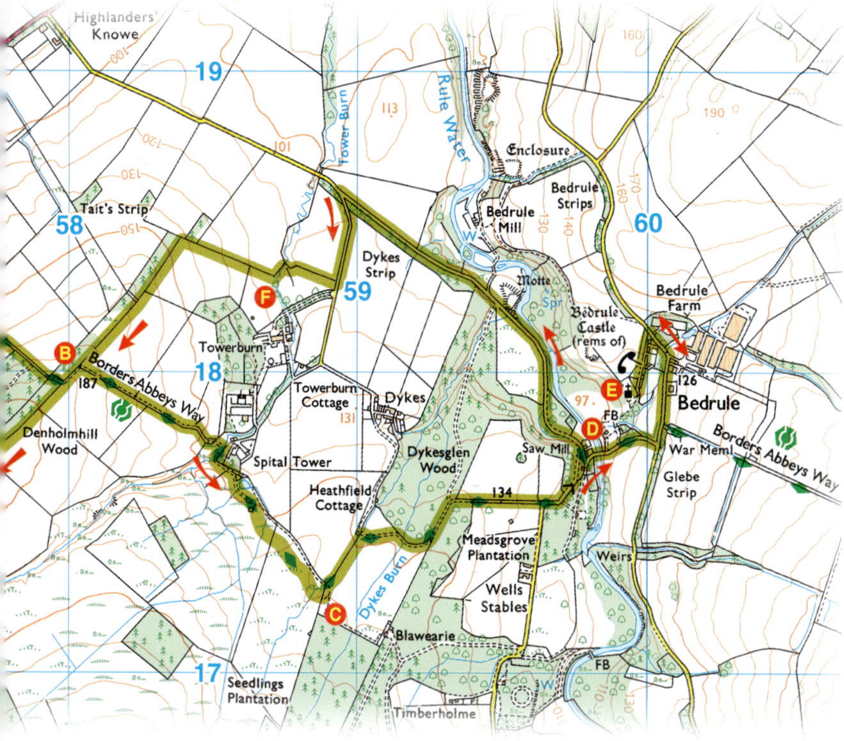

footbridge and turn left on a slight, rough path to another field **F**. The next part follows field edges with stiles over the fences.

Walk up the right side of two fields to a woodland strip. Looking to the right, you can see Fatlips Castle on wooded Minto Craigs and columnar Waterloo Monument further north-east on Peniel Heugh (Walk 8). Turn left at a fingerpost in the corner and walk up two fields with trees on your right. Rejoin the Borders Abbeys Way for 150 yards, crossing your outward route at **B**. Keep straight ahead along the field edges, with a line of beech on your right and rugged Rubers Law to the left, until you reach Gled'swing Strip **G**.

Go through a gate in a stone wall and bear right downhill on the edge of a felled wood. At the bottom, go right along a wall to a gap then follow a grassy path going half left, downhill towards Denholm. Further on the path becomes a track and leads down between gorse bushes to a minor road. Turn right, downhill, and just before Woodside (cottage) **H** go left down a path signed Denholm Dean (or miss it out and continue down the road).

At a T-junction, turn right downstream beside the burn. Go down steps and across a footbridge then up a flight of steps on the other side. Continue on the path, keeping ahead under dark trees to climb more steps. Then dip down across another footbridge over a side stream and continue until you return to the minor road further downhill. Turn left down the road which descends to the west end of the Green. ●

Leyden's Monument on Denholm Green

Lauder Common Circular

This walk starts along the Southern Upland Way then follows the traditional route of the Lauder Common Riding. Grassy tracks offer easy, but exposed walking. They gradually rise up to the crest of the extensive heather moorland, where views stretch for miles in all directions. The towers and turrets of Thirlestane Castle, one of the seven 'Great Houses in Scotland' can be seen to the east of the town.

If approaching from the north on the A68, turn right along Mill Wynd. If driving from the south, turn left, signed golf course, and follow Thirlestane Drive to the edge of town.

From the Southern Upland Way information board, walk through the car park and out on the far side by a post marked with the thistle symbol. The path gradually rises up to a bench by a gate where there is a good view back to Lauder and Thirlstane Castle. On the left here is a phone mast and just behind it lies Chester Hill Iron Age fort. Ignore a path signed to the right and continue gently climbing to pass below a copse on the skyline to a cairn **A**.

Keep ahead beside the golf course fence with wide views over the valley of Lauder Burn. At the fence corner continue straight ahead past a Southern Upland Way post. About 30 yards before a ladder stile in a wall, turn right downhill on a grassy track, leaving the Southern Upland Way. Soon, fork right, down a smaller path to a footbridge over Lauder Burn **B**.

Now walk straight up the grassy track ahead, signed Cuckoo Wood, passing under a wooden-poled power line. Ignore another track bearing right towards the clump of trees. At the top the track swings left to a gate in the wall surrounding Lauder Common, a large open area of heather moorland with red grouse and meadow pipits. Go through the gate **C**, turn left and walk downhill under pylons.

Cross a bridge then the Muircleugh farm road and keep ahead, rising uphill on a lesser track under more pylons. At a fork, go right to The Harefold wood, whose surrounding wall provides some shelter from the wind. Bear left at the corner and continue on a track running south-west. Just beyond the crossing point of two sets of wooden-poled power lines, turn right at a T-junction with a larger track **D**.

Reach the quiet B6362 road and go left along it for about ½ mile (800m) then turn right up a gravel track into a small

---

walk 21

Start
Lauder

Distance
7¾ miles (12.5km)

Height gain
900 feet (275m)

Approximate time
4 hours

Route terrain
Paths and tracks across open grassland and heather moor

Parking
Walkers' car park on west edge of Lauder

OS maps
Landranger 73 (Peebles, Galashiels & Selkirk), Explorer 338 (Galashiels, Selkirk & Melrose)

GPS waypoints
- NT 530 472
- **A** NT 521 463
- **B** NT 519 459
- **C** NT 512 462
- **D** NT 497 455
- **E** NT 487 456
- **F** NT 509 476
- **G** NT 521 482

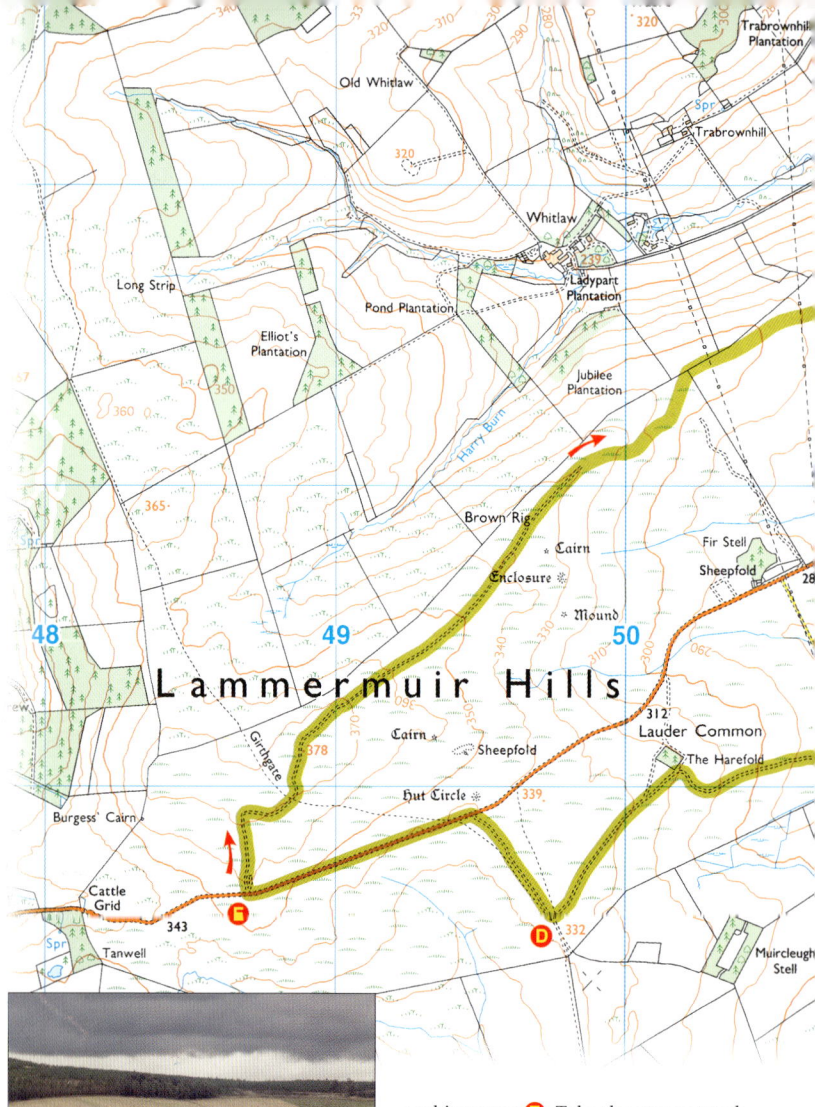

Approaching the sheepfold on the descent of Scarce Law

parking area **E**. Take the grassy track leading uphill away from the road and follow it hard right after 250 yards. The way then swings left up to the summit of the common (1,240 feet/378m) before bearing right to run north-east down Brown Rig with 360° views.

At a wall corner, go through a gate and keep ahead on grassier ground. Pass under the pylons again. Beyond a gate **F** by a junction of walls, continue down Scarce Law with a wall on your right. When the track goes through a gate in the wall by a sheepfold, keep ahead on a lesser track towards a metal tower, used for fire brigade practice.

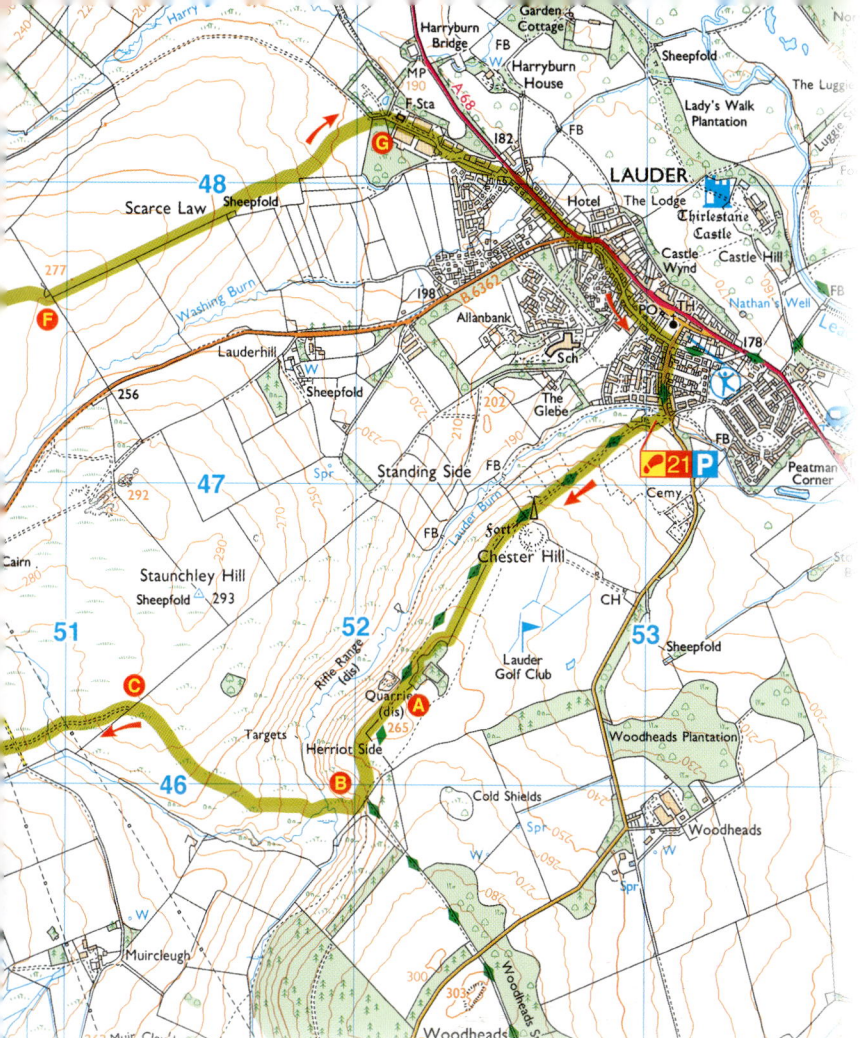

Lauder Common Riding

This event is held on the first Saturday in August. The tradition dates back to the 1600s, and involves riding the boundaries of Lauder Common to reinforce territorial rights and to bless the lands and affairs of the burgh. In the mid 1800s, the Town Council ordered an end to the festival as it had become too rowdy, with drunken racing of horses through the streets. It was revived in 1911 to mark the coronation of George V. The standard bearer who leads the cavalcade of horses is known as the Cornet.

Just before the tower meet a road and turn right through a gate to a junction by the fire station **G**.

Turn right and follow the pavement. At a brick-paved parking area fork right on a tarmac path that leads to the A68 by a garage. Turn right back into Lauder, passing the War Memorial at the Stow Road junction. Just beyond it fork right onto quieter Crofts Road. At a crossroads with Mill Wynd, turn right back to the car park (or left to visit the town centre).

LAUDER COMMON CIRCULAR • 63

Longer walks of 4½ hours and over

Crossing Chain Bridge over the River Tweed (Walk 28)

Dere Street and Mount Ulston

Walk in the footsteps of Roman soldiers on this route, which follows Dere Street, a road built by occupying Romans in AD 79–81, for almost 1¼ miles (2km). The walk begins from a car park just below ruined Jedburgh Abbey, follows part of the Borders Abbeys Way and also briefly meets St Cuthbert's Way. Most of the route is marked by horseshoe symbols as it is the Eastern Loop of the Jedburgh Horse Circular riding route. Fortunately the paths and tracks are well drained so are firm underfoot.

From the tourist information centre, leave the car park by the vehicle exit and cross the road. Turn right and go through an underpass beside the A68 road junction. Bear left to go over the old Canongate Bridge then left again up to a crossroads with a mini roundabout. Go straight over and, where the road bends right after Bountrees, fork left on a tarmac path that drops down onto the road to the school campus. Walk up it and in 50 yards cross over onto a gravel path that forks left under trees **A**.

The path runs above houses then past horse fields, before broadening to a track and going into woodland. At Hartrigge, go through a gate and bear right onto a drive that swings round Towerburn Stables to a road. Go left, downhill, and at a T-junction turn right, now on the Borders Abbeys Way. Soon fork right at a road junction before houses **B**.

The lane is tarmac up to Mount Ulston. Just before the house, fork left at an arrow onto a grassy path that runs parallel to the road with lovely views over Teviotdale to the Waterloo Monument on Peniel Heugh (Walk 8). The path climbs back up onto the previous line, continuing on an old trackway between a wood and open countryside. At a T-junction with a bench and fingerpost **C**, turn right up Dere Street, now on

walk 22

Start
Jedburgh

Distance
8½ miles (13.75km)

Height gain
900 feet (275m)

Approximate time
4½ hours

Route terrain
Good tracks and paths through woods and farmland

Parking
Canongate car park

OS maps
Landranger 80 (Cheviot Hills & Kielder Water), Explorer OL16 (The Cheviot Hills)

GPS waypoints
- NT 651 205
- **A** NT 655 206
- **B** NT 659 218
- **C** NT 668 233
- **D** NT 682 223
- **E** NT 673 203
- **F** NT 666 191
- **G** NT 656 204

Dere Street

This Roman road ran north from York at least as far as the Antonine Wall, which was built between the Firths of Forth and the Clyde in AD 142. It was used to move soldiers between forts and for trade. The road served Trimontium (see Walk 28) and crossed the Tweed at Leaderfoot by a stone bridge close to the present viaduct. In medieval times the section between Jedburgh and Edinburgh was known as the Royal Way. It connected ecclesiastical sites and was used by pilgrims and nobles.

St Cuthbert's Way.

Keep ahead when St Cuthbert's Way goes left. At a road crossing, go straight over, following Dere Street across a dip and back up again. At the top, turn right by a fingerpost (don't trip on the low bar of the horse gate) onto a narrower path through regenerating woodland **D**.

Beyond Roman Wood, keep ahead over a track into Grouse Wood. At a wooden gate, turn left along a track called Sandy Road to a junction. Go straight over a road, through a pedestrian gate and continue ahead with a hedge on your right. Go through a gate at the top, first looking back at the distant views, and then continue ahead with a fence on the left. The panorama opens out southwards to the Cheviots and Rubers Law. When a gate leads onto a road, walk to the right for 20 yards and then turn left on a path into Natural Wood **E**.

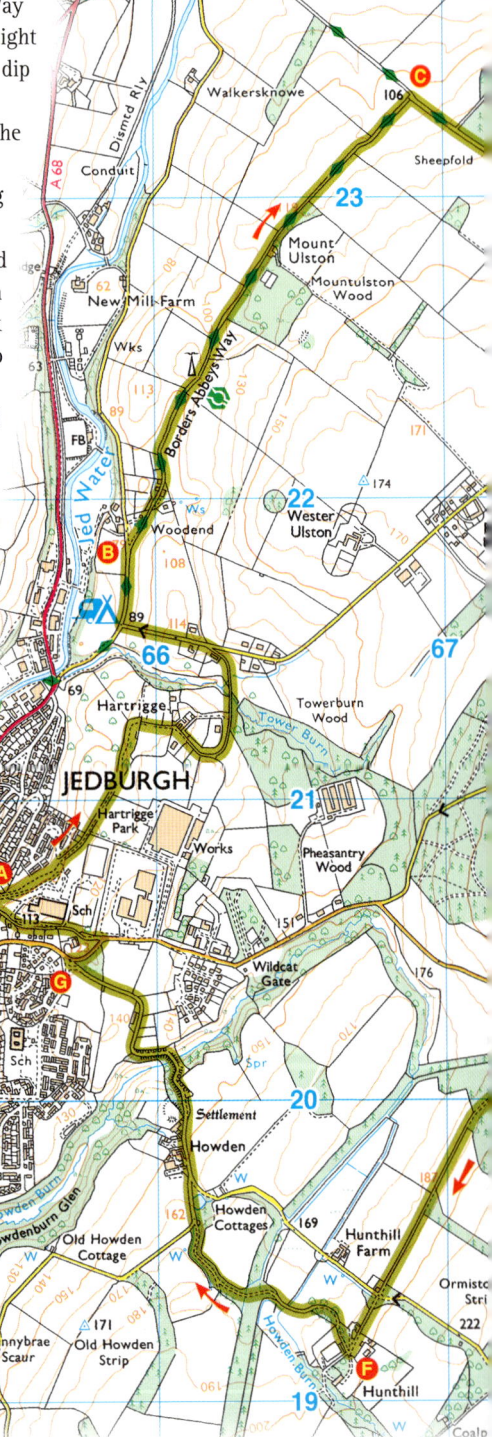

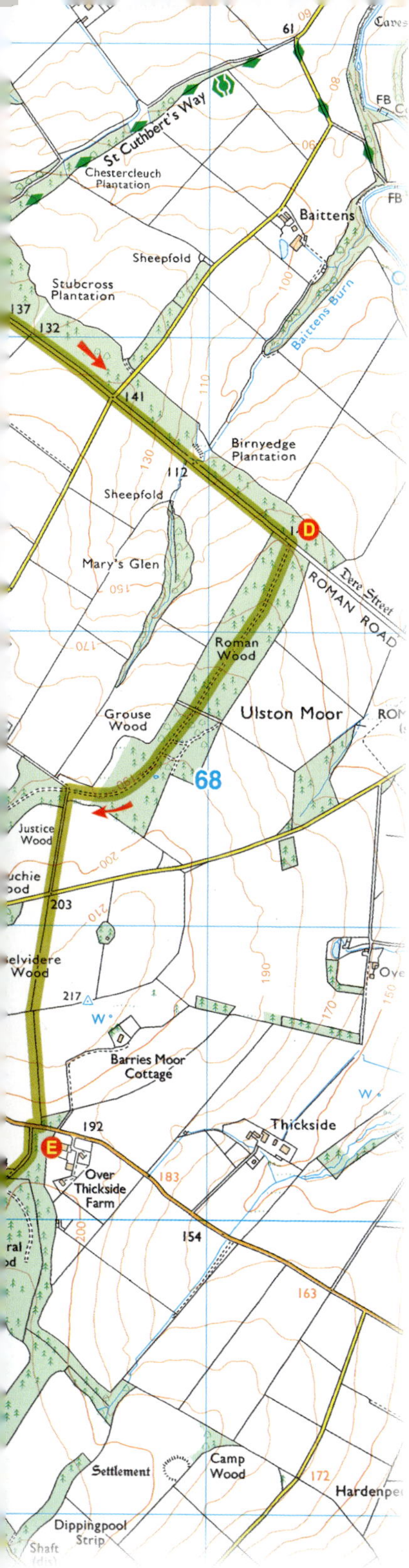

Jedburgh Abbey

King David I of Scotland founded a priory at Jedburgh in 1138 and later raised it to monastery then abbey status. It was dedicated to the Virgin Mary and its Augustinian canons are thought to have come originally from St Quentin Abbey in France. Being a centre of power and close to the border between Scotland and England, the abbey suffered major raids during the Wars of Independence. After the Protestant Reformation of 1560, the monks were allowed to stay and the abbey was used as the parish kirk for the reformed religion.

The path broadens to a track and runs between fields. On meeting a road, go straight over to walk between pillars and along the tarmac drive to Hunthill. In about 200 yards, before reaching a riding arena, turn right by a post with a yellow arrow into a wood **F**.

Keep ahead on the path winding downhill through trees. Bear right when a track joins from the left and follow it down to a cottage at Howden. Go through a gate and right along a road to a junction. Turn left downhill for 2/3 mile (a little over 1km). There is little traffic but it's safest to keep on the outside of the bends for visibility. At a road junction **G** go right and right again (or cut across the grass), as signed for the Jedburgh Circular.

Follow the pavement to the 30 mph sign and turn sharp left onto a sunken track. Keep straight ahead over a path by the high school. You emerge onto the road you left earlier, which curves left to the crossroads with a mini roundabout. Keep ahead to retrace your steps, via Canongate Bridge and the subway, to return to the car park.

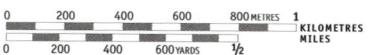

SCALE 1:25 000 or 2½ INCHES to 1 MILE 4CM to 1KM

walk 23

Cauldshiels Loch and the River Tweed

Start
Gun Knowe Loch, Tweedbank (on the eastern outskirts of Galashiels)

Distance
10 miles (16.3km)

Height gain
1,180 feet (360m)

Approximate time
5 hours

Route terrain
Lanes and clear paths

Parking
Car park at start

OS maps
Landranger 73 (Peebles, Galashiels & Selkirk), Explorer 338 (Galashiels, Selkirk & Melrose)

GPS waypoints
- NT 517 346
- Ⓐ NT 510 343
- Ⓑ NT 510 330
- Ⓒ NT 509 324
- Ⓓ NT 502 299
- Ⓔ NT 488 322
- Ⓕ NT 513 353

After a brief dalliance with the Tweed from a park at the edge of Galashiels, the route climbs from Abbotsford along forgotten country lanes to Cauldshiels Loch, a serene beauty spot tucked in the hills. An enjoyable saunter across upland grazing precedes an easy descent and return beside the river, a picturesque stretch much frequented by fishermen.

Gun Knowe Loch Previously a marsh where the townspeople would come to skate in winter, Gun Knowe Loch was created in 1978 and now attracts a wide range of waterbirds, including the seemingly resident mute swans.

Abbotsford House

From the car park follow the lakeside path in a clockwise direction. At a junction at the western corner, bear left, continuing past a football pitch toward trees at the far corner of the park. Picking up Borders Abbeys Way signs, pass behind houses along a steep wooded bank above the Tweed. Just before the main road, take a stepped path that dips beneath the bypass. Descend beyond into the wood, joining a broader track at the bottom. Climb to the B6360, emerging near the entrance to Abbotsford Ⓐ.

Cross to a narrow lane opposite, which rises through a verdant tunnel. Bending left in front of a cattle shed, carry on to a junction. Go right gaining more height, which opens a view towards the Eildon Hills. Wind past the picturesque pool at Abbotsmoss and, at the end, turn right again. Walk up the

CAULDSHIELS LOCH AND THE RIVER TWEED   69

> **Abbotsford** Abbotsford was the home of Sir Walter Scott, who became Scotland's greatest writer and father of the historical novel, *Rob Roy*, *Ivanhoe* and *Kenilworth* being among his best-known. He commissioned the splendid house in 1817 and lived there until his death in 1832.

lane for ¼ mile (400m) to reach a small parking area beside a crossing track **B**, where Cauldshiels Loch is signed to the left. Climb towards a forest plantation and swing within a fringe of ancient gnarled beech. Carry on beyond the track's end to the loch shore, a delightful spot for a picnic.

The onward path follows the shore to the right, soon meeting a broader path. Go right to a track **C** and turn left, climbing past more majestic beech trees over the shoulder of Dod. Out to the left is Cauldshiels Hill, its top crowned by an ancient defensive earthwork.

Swinging left by a corrugated barn, go through a couple of gates and continue beside a wall across upland grazing. Gently climbing, the way curves towards the transmitter mast on Lindean Moor, revealing views across the confluence of the Tweed and Ettrick valleys to the higher hills. Over the crest the path descends past another beech-fringed plantation, finally leaving the pastures along a short, rough track up to a lane **D**.

Falling steadily downhill, the quiet lane offers 1½ miles (2.4km) of easy walking, eventually ending at a junction with the A7. Cross to the minor lane opposite, which winds over a bridge spanning Ettrick Water. Formerly the main road, it runs beside the park of Sunderland Hall, across which there is a brief view of the elegant 18th-century mansion. Bending at the far end, the lane turns over a second bridge, this time crossing the River Tweed.

Immediately over the bridge, and just in front of a cycle track, go through a gate on the right **E** from which steps drop to the riverbank. A trod tacks the field edge past the confluence with Ettrick Water and beneath the modern road bridge. Before long, a track develops, which then moves from the river behind a small plantation to join the course of an old branch line that ran from Galashiels to Selkirk. Opened in 1856, it served the woollen mills for which the town was famous.

Walk on to meet a narrow lane that leads past the few houses at Boleside and then beside a small park, where you can rejoin the river. Later forced to return to the lane, carry on past a fork, just beyond which, a sign marks the Southern Upland Way branching back to the Tweed. Paralleling the lane, the way undulates through the trees, giving a glimpse to Abbotsford on the opposite bank.

Eventually the way passes beneath a high bridge carrying the main road. Remain by the river past a car park and then at the edge of a field until forced away by a tributary stream, Gala Water. Follow that up to a road and go right over a bridge. Walk to the top of a rise, there taking a shared-use path on the right **F** to cross the Tweed. The viaduct was built for the old Waverley Line and now has a new lease of life carrying the Borders Railway to Edinburgh, opened in 2015. Immediately over, drop to the right and walk from the bridge. Fork right beside a small substation to regain the riverbank, where, despite the proximity of the town, you might see an otter. After some 250 yards, leave the Tweed, turning towards a park. Keep ahead across the open playing fields, finally returning to Gun Knowe Loch. You can skirt round it either left or right back to the car park.

Kirk Yetholm and the Halterburn Valley

The 18th-century Border Hotel is a welcome sight for weary walkers completing the Pennine Way. This ramble combines the alternative routes of the trail's final leg, heading out on the long ridge from White Law to Black Hag and returning down the deep valley of Halter Burn. Although the paths are generally clear, inexperienced walkers should choose a fine day.

The border between Scotland and England below Whitelaw Nick

walk 24

Start
Kirk Yetholm

Distance
8½ miles (13.7km)

Height gain
1,985 feet (605m)

Approximate time
4¾ hours

Route terrain
Reasonably clear, but remote moorland paths and tracks

Parking
Around the green at Kirk Yetholm

OS maps
Landranger 74 (Kelso & Coldstream), Explorer OL16 (The Cheviot Hills)

GPS waypoints
- NT 827 281
- Ⓐ NT 839 276
- Ⓑ NT 853 269
- Ⓒ NT 858 235
- Ⓓ NT 846 256

Signed as the Pennine and St Cuthbert's ways, High Street climbs from the village green over the shoulder of Staerough Hill into the Halter Burn Valley. At a cattle grid Ⓐ, drop left to a footbridge spanning the stream and head up beside a wall. Just before the end, strike right across the bracken-clad flank of Green Humbleton. Curving from Shielknowe Burn, gain height to a fork where St Cuthbert's Way goes left. However, keep ahead with the Pennine Way, the path soon levelling onto Stob Rig and approaching a stone wall that marks the boundary between Scotland and England. Ignore the gate and stile into England Ⓑ and instead bear right beside the wall.

The path dips abruptly across the head of Witchcleuch Burn, rising sharply beyond to Whitelaw Nick. Cross a wall and bear left beside the frontier, ascending to the summit of White Law. At a junction of fences there, ignore the gate and swing right with the ongoing boundary. As the path falls once more there is a view ahead to The Cheviot.

Beyond a saddle, the way progresses steadily along Steer Rig.

KIRK YETHOLM AND THE HALTERBURN VALLEY ● 71

> **Pennine Way** The 268-mile (431-km) Pennine Way was the first long-distance national trail to be established in the country and was opened in 1965. Conceived by Tom Stephenson 30 years earlier, it rambles across some of the wildest landscape in the Pennines between Edale in Derbyshire and Kirk Yetholm, just inside the Scottish border.

Approaching the final ascent onto Steerrig Knowe, a prominent ditch and embankment crossing the path marks an ancient boundary. After another gate the gradient eases, shortly arriving at a junction of fences and wall. This is the highest point of the walk and affords a grand panorama across the northern Cheviot Hills. Through the gate, the path leaves the comforting guidance of the fence, bearing right past a waymark and dropping to a junction beside a signpost **C**.

The Pennine Way low-level route is signed back right, falling above the source of Rowhope Burn to a gate. Beyond, the path loses height sharply above the headwaters of Curr Burn before passing through another gate into the upper reaches of the Halter Burn Valley. The way now descends more easily towards Old Halterburnhead. Reaching the corner of a wall, follow it past the ruined steading, which huddles in the shelter of a clump of storm-ravaged trees.

Just beyond, the Pennine Way swings left, continuing down the valley to Burnhead. Approaching the farm, watch for a sign **D** indicating a trod on the right that winds down to a sturdy wooden bridge spanning the stream. Go left to a kissing-gate and accompany the wall above the farm. Over a stile beside a gate, walk out to a track and follow it down the valley. Shortly after passing the cottages of Halterburn, pick up your outward route at the cattle grid **A** to return over the hill to Kirk Yetholm. ●

Cattle graze the slopes of Steerrig Knowe

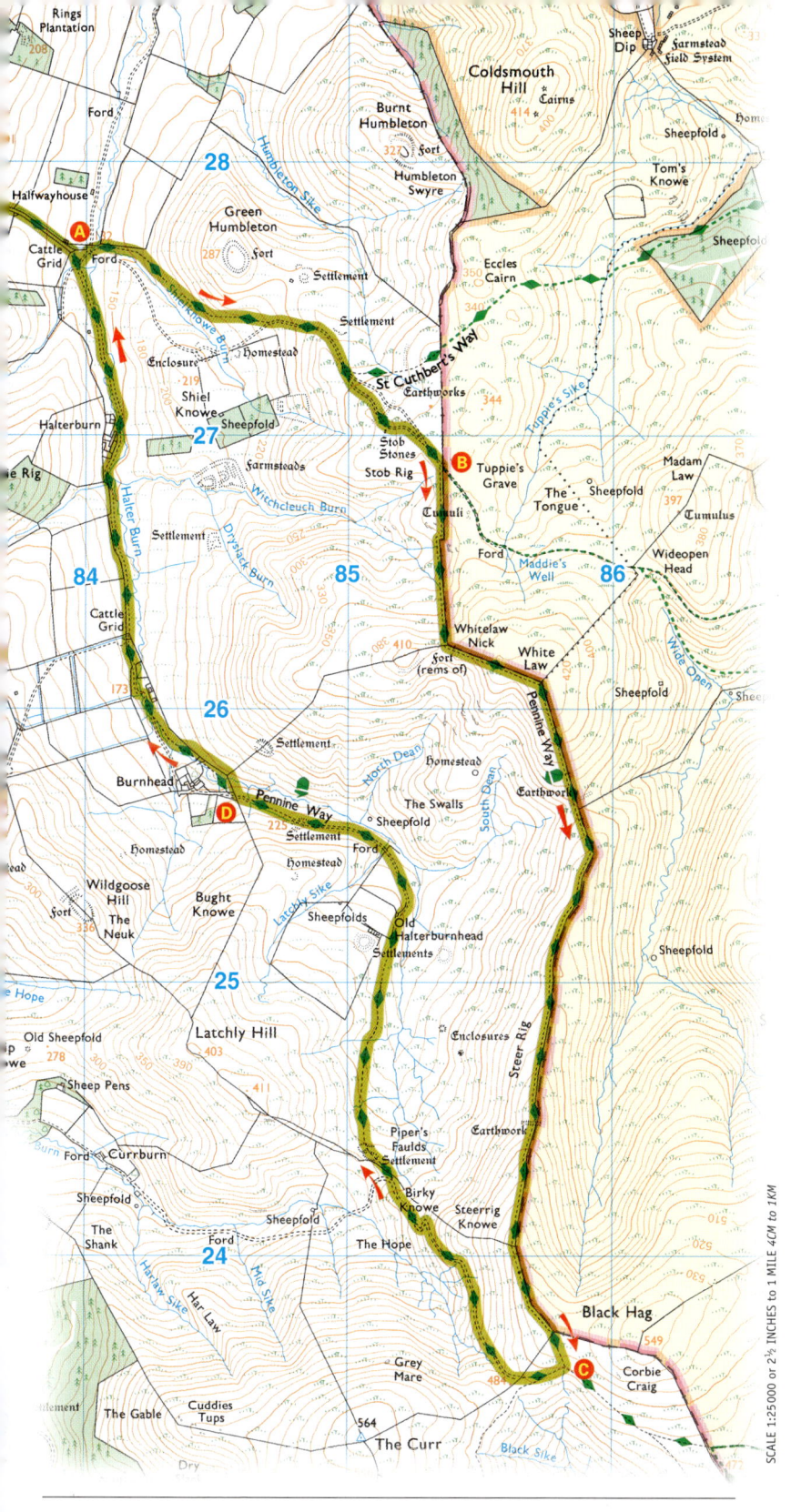

KIRK YETHOLM AND THE HALTERBURN VALLEY • 73

walk 25

St Mary's Loch Circuit

Start
South end of St Mary's Loch

Distance
9½ miles (15.3km)

Height gain
655 feet (200m)

Approximate time
4¾ hours

Route terrain
Fields, wooded paths, tracks and stretches of road verge

Parking
Car park on A708 by Glen Café or at the two picnic sites on the other side of the road

OS maps
Landranger 79 (Hawick & Eskdale), Explorer 330 (Moffat & St Mary's Loch)

GPS waypoints
- NT 238 204
- Ⓐ NT 242 212
- Ⓑ NT 255 226
- Ⓒ NT 270 239
- Ⓓ NT 267 247
- Ⓔ NT 265 239
- Ⓕ NT 254 236
- Ⓖ NT 244 231
- Ⓗ NT 240 222

St Mary's Loch is the largest natural loch in Scottish Borders. It lies deep in the hills at the head of the beautiful Yarrow Valley. A weir helps to control the river's flow and protect downstream Selkirk from flooding. This walk follows the Ring of the Loch route, which uses the Southern Upland Way along the east shore and an old drove road above the west side. Near the car park is a large, white monument to the self-taught poet, novelist and essayist James Hogg, known as 'The Ettrick Shepherd'.

> **St Mary's Kirkyard**
> No sign remains of St Mary's Church, which dated back to the late 1200s, but its graveyard has a long history that mingles fact and fable. Legend has it that William Wallace was proclaimed Guardian of Scotland here and that it contains the graves of the lovers who feature in the traditional ballard *The Douglas Tragedy*. In the 17th century, outlawed Covenanters worshipped here and outdoor services are still held each summer.

The Ring of the Loch route is well signed with wooden fingerposts and red disks with arrows. The uphill legs to ancient St Mary's Kirkyard and medieval Dryhope Tower (where a footbridge is currently closed over a burn that can be tricky to cross when in spate) can be omitted, saving about 2 miles (3.2km). If the loch is exceptionally high, it may be necessary to stay on the road verge rather than use shore paths after Ⓗ.

Leave the car park and cross the stone bridge between St Mary's Loch and Loch of the Lowes. Pass **Tibbie Shiel's Inn** and an information board then go left through a kissing-gate on the Southern Upland Way, following a driveway to St Mary's Loch Sailing Club. Pass on the loch side of the building then go over a stile and follow a path by the shore.

Pass the end of a wall Ⓐ into March Wood, a remnant of the Great Ettrick Forest. Cross a plank bridge over a stream then go through a gate with a stile beside it. Follow the path below a forest, some of which is felled. Low-growing willow covers the steep bank below the path. Beyond a shingle point, leave the forest by a gate and stile.

At a wall Ⓑ go over a stile (or through two gates) into young

Upturned rowing boat at Bowerhope

woodland below a field. Another gate leads through more woodland and over a bridge across a stream. Leave the wood by a further gate and walk beside the shore across a sheep field with Bowerhope on the right. Join the Bowerhope drive by a gate and stile, and continue along it above the shore. Keep ahead when a forest road joins from above.

At the end of the loch, pass a barrier by a weir then cross a bridge over the river to two fingerposts by a phone mast ●. To visit Dryhope Tower, turn right on the Southern Upland Way through a gate with a stile. Stay by the river across a field then turn left beside a wall. Near the road, go right through two gates with a footbridge in between. Keep ahead then cross a stile to the A708 just beyond another gate. Cross with care to a stile and gate and keep ahead up a grassy track. Go through two gates and stay beside the wall to another gate onto a track.

Turn left through a gate and down the track towards a farm until level with the tower then cross the burn (the footbridge here is currently unsafe and closed). Dryhope Tower ● is always open (push the door hard) and a metal spiral staircase gives access to the roof for the view. Return the same way to ● and follow Ring of the Loch signs through a gate. By the weir, another gate then a stile lead to the shore path. Go over a stile at the end of a wall and turn right between it and a fence.

> **Dryhope Tower** Built by the Scott family, this four-storey tower house dates from the 16th century. It is typical of the period of Border Reivers, when armed and mounted gangs attacked homes and farms to steal livestock and valuables. Landowning families needed easily-defended homes to protect themselves from raids by neighbours, and often as a base for their own raids.

ST MARY'S LOCH CIRCUIT ● 75

Beyond a kissing-gate, access the road by a sliding gate and stile and turn left over a bridge.

At the foot of Kirkstead drive **E**, go over a stile by a fingerpost then head half right over a plank bridge. Go through the leftmost of the two gates ahead, onto an old drove road. Follow this parallel to the road. Beyond a metal gate, cross a ford and keep forward until a fingerpost points right for St Mary's Kirkyard. Climb a grassy path through bracken and cross a footbridge just

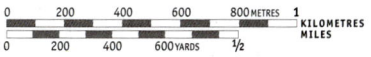

ST MARY'S LOCH CIRCUIT 77

St Mary's Kirkyard

before the walled enclosure. A gate by an information board F gives access and a bench seat has lovely views of the loch.

Continue across a narrow burn in a gully onto a green path that leads back down to the drove road. To the right, keep along it until the edge of Cappercleuch, where it meets the road at a gate. Cross carefully then go down a path and over a footbridge G behind the green village hall. Beyond buildings the path rejoins the road. Continue on the verge and pass the Megget Reservoir turning.

Cross Megget Bridge and keep on past a wood and a field until the road comes close to the loch. By a post H, follow the arrow down the slope to the loch shore. Walk below a wood, returning to the road just before a boathouse. Beyond the walled garden of Rodono, go left at a post back to the shore.

Rejoin the road by a wall before Summerhope. Beyond the buildings the path angles back to the shore, initially with a wall on the left then along the edge of the water below trees. Keep ahead at the end of the loch to join the road by the fingerpost passed at the start. A path opposite the road junction leads up to the James Hogg monument, where his statue gazes over the land he loved.

The Megget valley from the east shore of St Mary's Loch

Traquair and Minch Moor

Beginning from the forestry car park, the route winds through the Traquair estate to the village, there joining the Southern Upland Way along an old track onto Minch Moor. The return is through the extensive forest aproning the northern slopes, where felling has opened spectacular views. The trek ends in an easy stretch above the River Tweed.

walk 26

Start
Innerleithen

Distance
10 miles (16km)

Height gain
1,505 feet (460m)

Approximate time
5¼ hours

Route terrain
Good forest tracks and quiet lanes

Parking
Car park at edge of village

OS maps
Landranger 73 (Peebles, Galashiels & Selkirk), Explorer 337 (Peebles & Innerleithen)

GPS waypoints
- NT 335 357
- Ⓐ NT 330 346
- Ⓑ NT 360 335
- Ⓒ NT 358 330
- Ⓓ NT 368 332
- Ⓔ NT 369 349
- Ⓕ NT 369 345
- Ⓖ NT 367 368

Through a gate opposite the car park entrance, follow a path away across meadow. At the end, swing left through a couple of gates onto a broader track. After 50 yards, bear off right as the path resumes, winding behind Traquair Lodge to meet a driveway to the big house by a bridge. The onward path, however, continues opposite, later crossing another track.

> **Traquair House** Originally a 12th-century royal hunting lodge and forest court, Traquair is said to be the oldest inhabited castle in Scotland. The present building dates from the 15th century when a degree of peace settled on the area. The family remained true to the Scottish throne and following a visit by Bonnie Prince Charlie in 1744, the earl closed the Bar Gates, vowing they would never be reopened until a Stuart was crowned in London.

Emerging at Traquair by a war memorial Ⓐ, diagonally cross the main road to a climbing lane, signed the Southern Upland Way. Where the lane bends right to Birkinshaw, keep ahead to Minch Moor. Later swinging left towards the sprawling forest, carry on up at the edge of the trees, before long passing a timber bothy set back in a clearing. Walking on, cross a forest road to intercept a second one, higher up.

Take the rightmost of the two paths opposite, rising through more saplings towards the upper slopes of Minch Moor. Eventually breaking from the trees, look to the slopes below, where circular clearings in the heather are an artwork entitled *Point of Resolution* by Charles Poulson. Keep an eye open too for wildlife; buzzard, grouse, curlew and golden plover inhabit the moor, while among those seeking shelter in the trees are siskin and crossbill. Roe deer wander within the forest and in spring you may hear a cuckoo.

Farther along on the right is the Cheese Well, a trickling spring marked with a stone slab. Drovers used to make

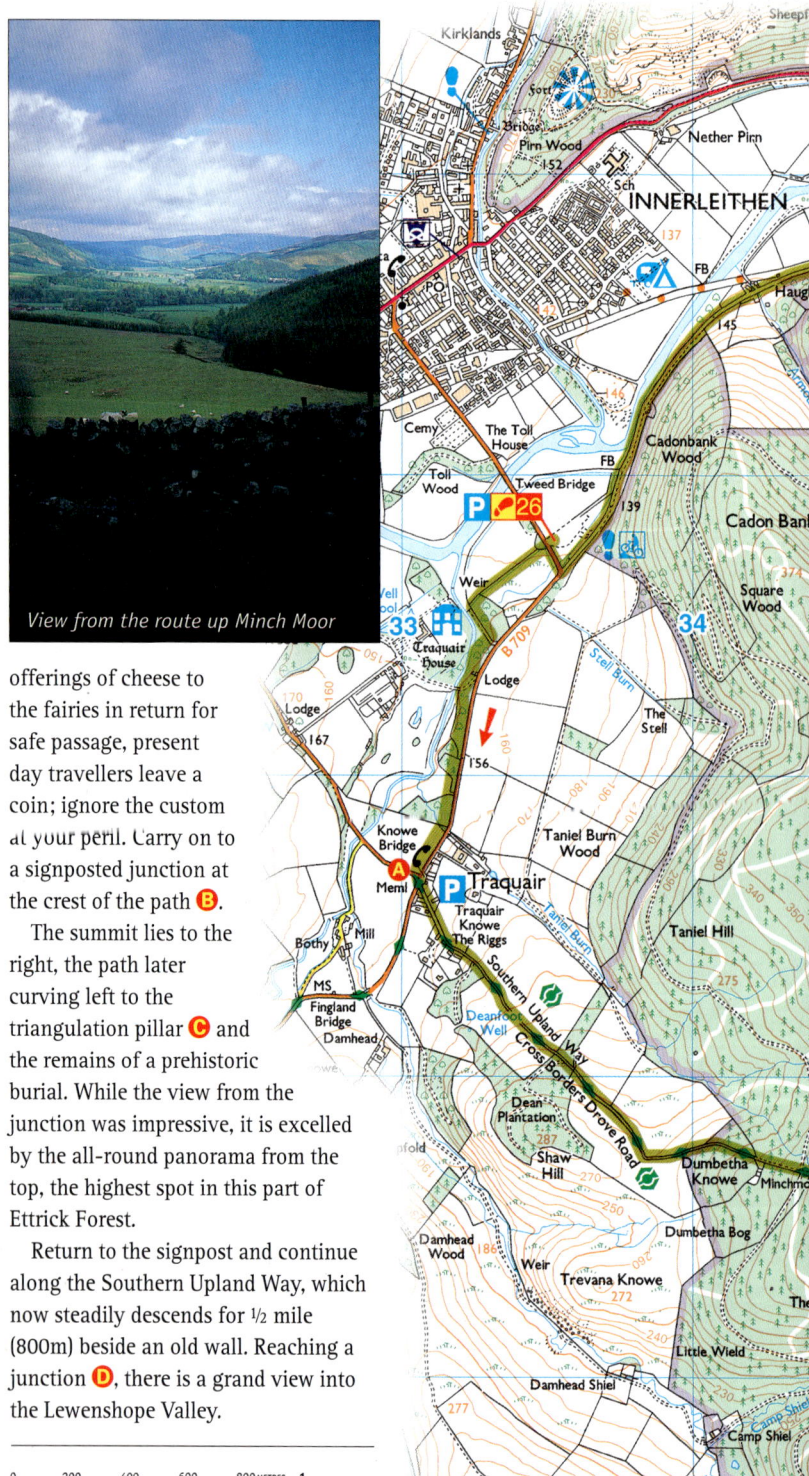

View from the route up Minch Moor

offerings of cheese to the fairies in return for safe passage, present day travellers leave a coin; ignore the custom at your peril. Carry on to a signposted junction at the crest of the path **B**.

The summit lies to the right, the path later curving left to the triangulation pillar **C** and the remains of a prehistoric burial. While the view from the junction was impressive, it is excelled by the all-round panorama from the top, the highest spot in this part of Ettrick Forest.

Return to the signpost and continue along the Southern Upland Way, which now steadily descends for ½ mile (800m) beside an old wall. Reaching a junction **D**, there is a grand view into the Lewenshope Valley.

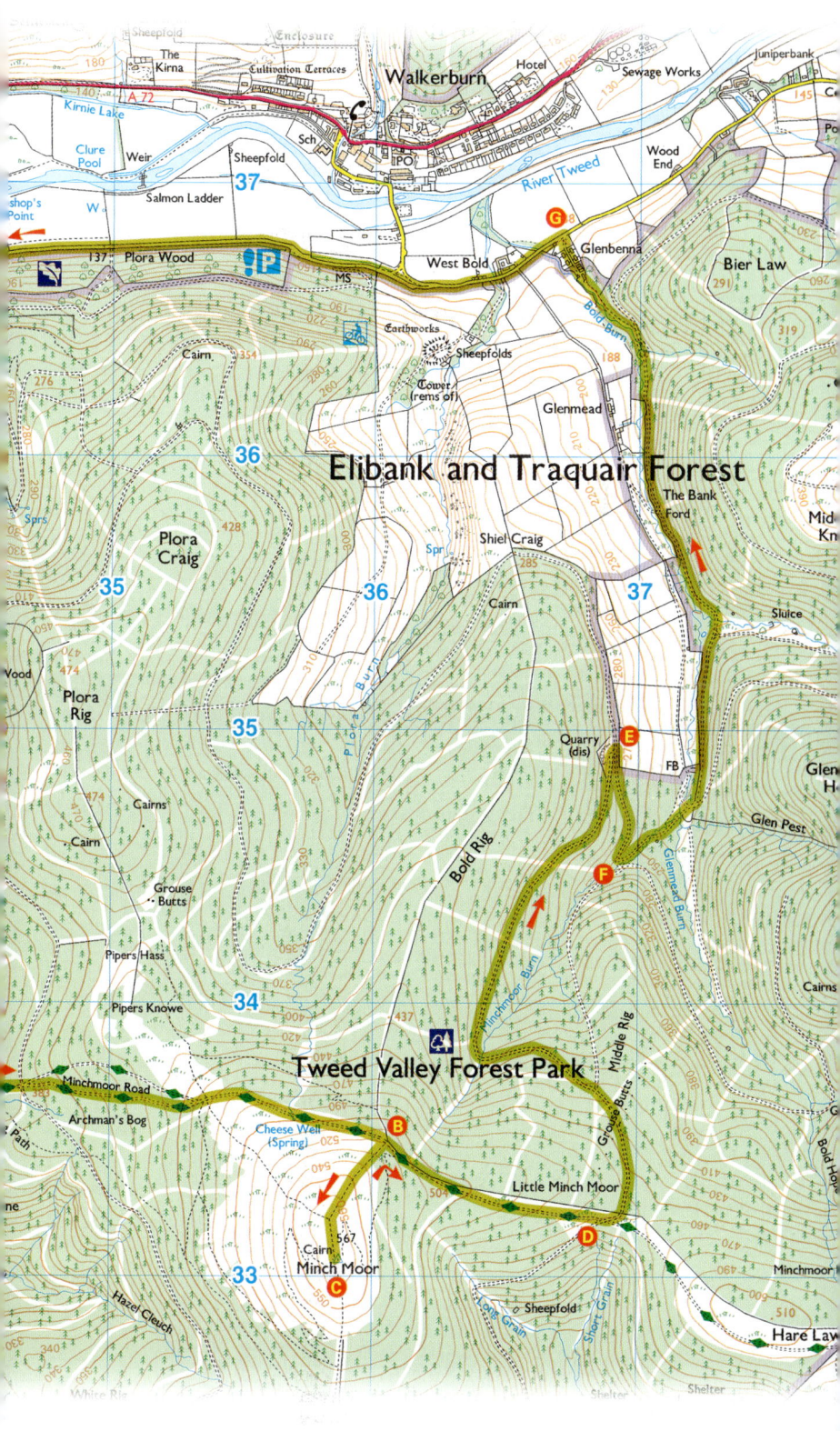

TRAQUAIR AND MINCH MOOR • 81

Looking down from Minch Moor into the Tweed Valley

Leaving the Southern Upland Way, take the rough road to the left. After a brief climb it settles into a long descent through the forest below Bold Rig. After 1½ miles (2.4km), views open into the Bold Burn Valley and the dirt road reaches a junction **E**. Go sharp right, dropping another ¼ mile (400m) to a second junction **F**. Now, turn left beside Minchmoor Burn and remain with the main track as it runs along the base of the scenic valley above Bold Burn. On the far side of the Tweed Valley is Cairn Hill, and then, as you leave the trees behind, you can see back over Bold Rig to Minch Moor.

Eventually the track meets a lane **G** at the foresters' hamlet of Glenbenna. Go left and later keep ahead past the junction to Walkerburn. Continue below the steep slopes of Traquair Forest all the way back to the car park.

Yarrowford, Minchmoor Road and Three Brethren

The majority of this walk follows two long-distance paths. It ascends the hills via the historic Minchmoor Road, which is part of the Cross Borders Drove Road, and then runs along their crest on the Southern Upland Way to the Three Brethren. These are three 8-foot-high (2.4m) cairns situated at the junction of three estates. The high level walking offers spectacular views and the ridge is also popular with mountain bikers who ascend from the Tweed Valley in the north.

This route circuits an area where woodland is being planted and a path network created. New paths are encountered near the start, but left behind after **B**.

Cross the road and walk 30 yards to the left to take the turning that is signed Yarrowford Village Hall. Pass the red corrugated steel hall and keep ahead past a play area. Beyond a row of wooden garages, fork right on a track with a green sign for Minchmoor. Follow the track for 100 yards then turn left up a new path that angles back up the hill. Cross a steep track and go through a gate in a wall, continuing on the path that soon bends right up to the top of the forest. You can continue on it for ¼ mile (400m), but for fine views go right at the next bend and through a gate **A** at the top of the steep track onto open pasture with a wide view over Gruntly Burn.

Turn left to walk up the grassy ridge with a wall on your left. After the first field, go through a gate where the surfaced path emerges from the forest. By a bench **B**, after the next field, the new path descends to the right. Leave it here and continue on the Cross Borders Drove Road beside the wall, staying on the hill crest. This grassy path soon bends right then left, following the wall, to a gate in a fence. It continues ahead up Hangingshaw Rig, initially with a fence on the right. Pass through a gap in a wall and dip down to a gate in a fence **C**, where the Minchmoor Road enters the open ground at the top of a forest.

The path skirts the flank of Brown Knowe, gently ascending for nearly 1½ miles (2.3km). It meets the Southern Upland Way

walk 27

Start
Yarrowford

Distance
9½ miles (15.1km)

Height gain
1,785 feet (545m)

Approximate time
5½ hours

Route terrain
Open hill ridges with earth and grass paths; through woodland lower down

Parking
Lay-by on A708 in Yarrowford, by the phone box

OS maps
Landranger 73 (Peebles, Galashiels & Selkirk), Explorer 337 (Peebles & Innerleithen) and Explorer 338 (Galashiels, Selkirk & Melrose)

GPS waypoints
- NT 408 299
- **A** NT 406 303
- **B** NT 400 305
- **C** NT 392 311
- **D** NT 379 327
- **E** NT 402 327
- **F** NT 421 318
- **G** NT 432 319
- **H** NT 418 305

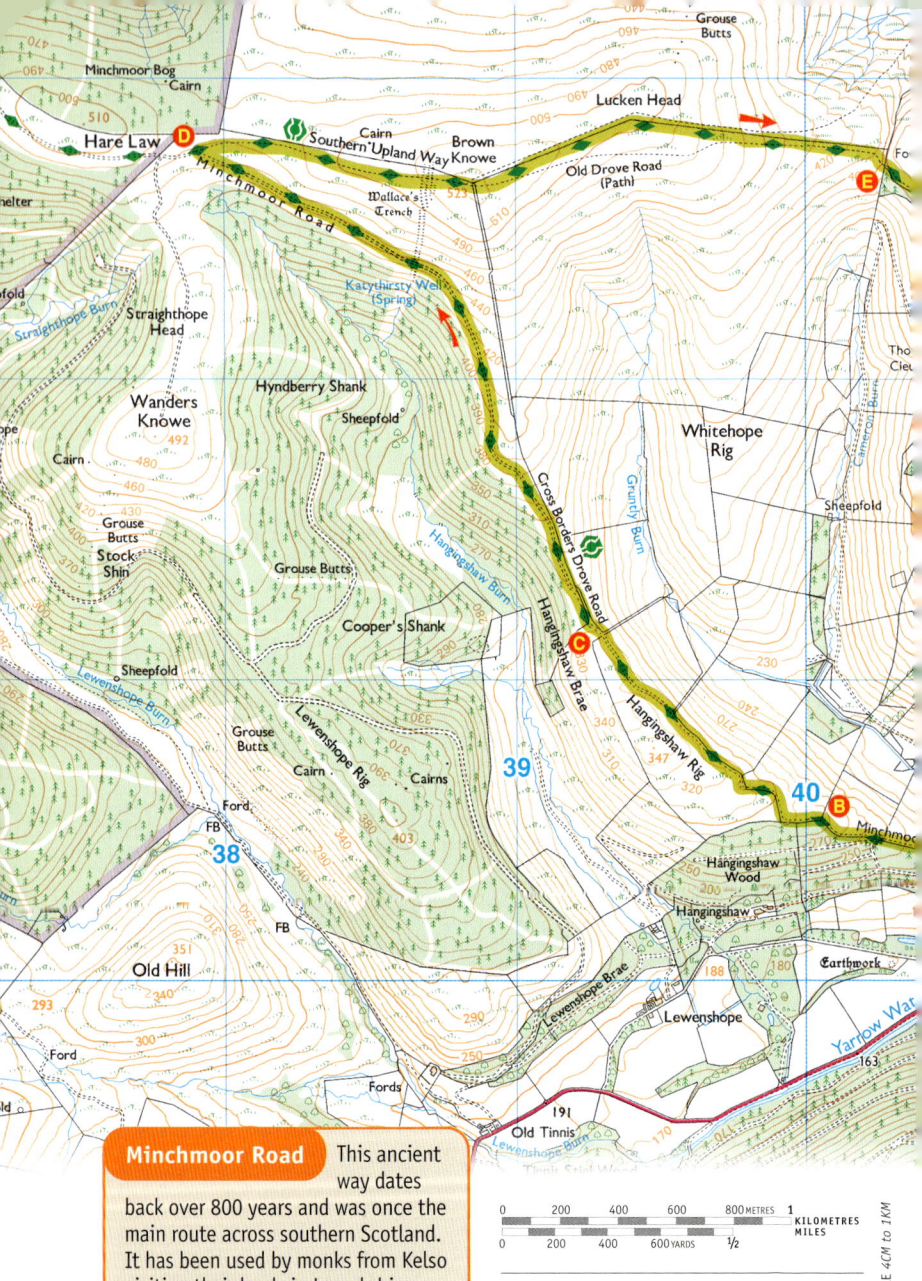

Minchmoor Road This ancient way dates back over 800 years and was once the main route across southern Scotland. It has been used by monks from Kelso visiting their lands in Lanarkshire and by drovers to herd cattle and sheep to market. In olden times the river valleys were boggy and thickly wooded, so it was easier to keep to higher, drier ground.

at a fingerpost **D**, where you turn sharp right. Continue uphill, passing through the bank and ditch of Wallace's Trench shortly before reaching the summit of Brown Knowe. The cairn on top marks the high point of the walk at 1,715 feet/523m. Continue ahead over a stile and downhill with a fence to the left. The views are panoramic and you can see Clovenfords nestled in the hills to the north-east.

Descend Lucken Head and in the dip at the bottom cross a stile and gate **E**. This place is named Four Lords Lands

The Southern Upland Way runs along the hill tops

YARROWFORD, MINCHMOOR ROAD AND THREE BRETHREN • 85

because it was the meeting point of four estates. The path skirts a hill, passing above a line of mature Scots pines, and then dips down to another stile and gate. It then curves round the left side of Broomy Law to a further stile and gate. About 250 yards further on, a fingerpost **F** points right for Yarrowford, over a ladder stile across the wall (a potential shortcut to **H**).

Keep ahead on the Southern Upland Way, soon entering a forest by a gate and stile. The path leads past a bench and along the top edge to the Three Brethren and a trig point **G**. After enjoying the view, stretching east to the Eildon Hills, turn right through a gate in the fence running between the tall cairns and descend a path southwards. As the forest off to the left curves away, look for a narrow path bearing right. If you miss this shortcut, turn right at the crossroads with a small path a little further down. This takes you through a gate and stile then across a wet area feeding Long Philip Burn. The path rises over a saddle behind Foulshiels Hill and becomes a track that descends steeply towards Broadmeadows.

On meeting a wood **H**, go right then left across sections of boardwalk along its top edge. Cross a footbridge, go through a wooden gate then turn left through a metal gate. Descend just inside birch woodland. At Broadmeadows, previously a Youth Hostel and now a private house, go through a little gate and down a few steps then continue ahead. Take care on the narrow path, which curves right under mature trees, high above Old Broadmeadows Burn then above the Yarrow with a sheer drop below. Beyond a rhododendron tunnel, emerge onto a tarmac lane and turn left down it. At the main road turn right for 600 yards back to the start, using the verge when there is oncoming traffic. ●

The Three Brethren

Southern Upland Way and Leaderfoot

walk 28

Start
Melrose

Distance
10¼ miles (16.4km)

Height gain
1,280 feet (390m)

Approximate time
5½ hours

Route terrain
Paths and tracks through farmland and woodland

Parking
Abbey car park

OS maps
Landranger 73 (Peebles, Galashiels & Selkirk), Explorer 338 (Galashiels, Selkirk & Melrose)

GPS waypoints
- NT 547 341
- Ⓐ NT 545 345
- Ⓑ NT 534 349
- Ⓒ NT 536 361
- Ⓓ NT 545 379
- Ⓔ NT 558 382
- Ⓕ NT 572 371
- Ⓖ NT 578 364
- Ⓗ NT 577 347
- Ⓙ NT 562 342

This walk offers an excellent leg stretch and a peaceful day in scenic countryside. Although long, it doesn't climb very high and the ascent is steady rather than steep. The route starts and finishes beside the broad River Tweed and crosses two pedestrian bridges over it. It heads north on the Southern Upland Way and returns through the Eildon and Leaderfoot National Scenic Area. Here it enters the intimate wooded valley of Leader Water then passes the splendid Leaderfoot Viaduct and Trimontium Roman Fort.

The Southern Upland Way long-distance route is followed from Ⓐ to Ⓓ and is marked by posts with a thistle symbol. The Leader Water Path, developed by Earlston Paths Group, is used from Ⓕ to Ⓗ. It is part of a network marked by yellow arrows and fingerposts.

Facing the Abbey, walk left along the pavement and turn first left, by a brown sign for Harmony Garden. Keep ahead then beyond Melrose Rugby Club turn right up a path signed for Chain Bridge (and other places). When you reach the River Tweed, turn right at a fingerpost signed Southern Upland Way then go left over Chain Bridge Ⓐ.

On the far side, turn hard left to follow a path along the riverbank. Walk beside the Tweed for ¾ mile (1.2km) until the path slopes uphill to the Gattonside road. Turn left on the pavement to the 40 mph speed limit sign then turn right up a track Ⓑ.

At a road junction, go straight ahead up a no-through road, signed Housebyres Farm. Where the road bends left, keep ahead on a track. Beyond a stile by a gated gap, keep ahead where another track Ⓒ forks to the right signed Earlston 2 miles.

Continue on the Southern Upland Way through woodland. Where the trees on the left end, a pile of stones called Deadwife's Grave can be seen across a field. Continue up the ascending track between hedges to a gate and stile then keep ahead across open pasture with a wall on the left. A stream flows under the track by a gate. Enjoy expanding views as you rise up the next field.

Pass a stile and gate, where Easter Housebyres Farm lies in the green valley below. Continue on the level then go through a gate and woodland strip above the farm, keeping ahead where a

88 • WALK 28

SOUTHERN UPLAND WAY AND LEADERFOOT 89

The Leaderfoot Viaduct over the Tweed

track goes left. Go through two gates by Housebyres Moss and keep ahead with a hedge on your left.

About 75 yards after a stream flows under the track, come to a large pile of rocks and a post indicating that the Southern Upland Way curves to the left **D**. Fork right towards the forest above and enter it by a gate at its low point.

Fallen trees block the old trackway through the forest so, as soon as you have passed initial gorse bushes, go right and pick up a deer trod just inside the boundary wall. On the edge of the mature trees, curve left following their edge and step into a field where a fallen tree holds down the fence (which could be electrified). Walk left round the outside of the forest. At its tip go through a gate onto a track and turn right along it. Go through five gates, many of which may be open, and past a sheep-handling area then walk gently downhill.

By a phone mast **E** on the corner of a wood, turn right through a gate and walk down a less used, gorse-lined track. At the next wood, turn left on a vehicle track and follow it downhill to a gate onto a minor road. Turn right along it for almost ¾ mile (1.1km), keeping ahead at a junction signed left for Earlston.

On meeting the A68, cross with care to a fingerpost and descend a path signed Leaderfoot 2½ miles **F**. Go down steps to a T-junction and turn right over a footbridge and through a kissing-gate. Walk through woodland, turning left up steps then along a fenced path high above Leader Water, which you follow for the next 2 miles (3.2km) or so, up and down a winding path.

Pass a footbridge over the river signed Leaderfoot via Jubilee Path (an alternative route down the other bank) and keep ahead following signs for Leaderfoot via Drygrange. Curve right up steps to a gate then bear left between fields. Three benches above Cowdenknowes make a good resting place. Beyond two gates, re-enter woodland and keep left at a fingerpost, soon crossing a footbridge over a stream. At the riverbank go through a kissing-gate **G** and keep left by the river.

Continue up steps with gates at bottom and top, along a field edge and through another kissing-gate. The path turns downhill then goes sharp right by a bench overlooking the river. Cross a footbridge over a side stream then go uphill into a sycamore plantation with a sign about woodland wildlife.

At a fingerpost, go left, keeping left down steps past Grange Community Orchard. Further on, walk round the foot of a high wall and continue above the river. The path arcs round a stream valley into conifers. Go left at a post with a yellow arrow and along the riverbank to a road ⓗ beside a stone road bridge.

Go right on a path signed Leaderfoot Bridge, which crosses the road in 10 yards. Follow it down steps and right before climbing steps to a lay-by. Walk under the A68 flyover and immediately turn left over old Drygrange Bridge, signed Newstead 1 mile, and enjoy a superb view of Leaderfoot Viaduct over the Tweed.

On the far side, turn right on a road closed to traffic. Just after passing under the viaduct, a path on the left signed Broomhill leads to a wooden tower overlooking Trimontium Roman Fort. Continue along the tarmac passing more information boards about the fort and a platform overlooking the amphitheatre. The Trimontium Memorial is at the crest of the road and beyond is another platform by the Roman baths and mansion.

At a road junction (with two more information boards) keep ahead and walk through Newstead. At Eddy Road

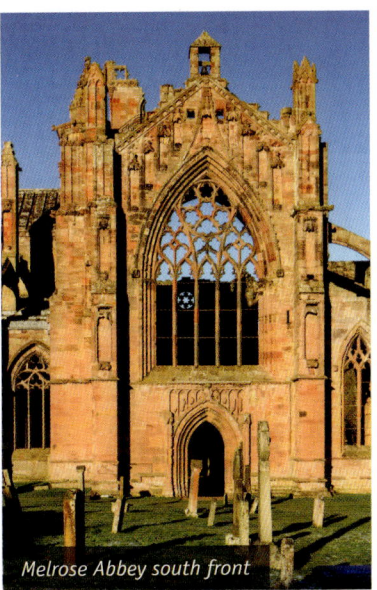

Melrose Abbey south front

Trimontium

Named after the three peaks of Melrose's Eildon Hills, this Roman camp was occupied for over a century from AD 79. It was the largest Roman fort and settlement north of Hadrian's Wall. The Roman road Dere Street ran through the camp and crossed the Tweed by a bridge at Leaderfoot. The walk passes many interpretation boards and there is a fascinating Trimontium Museum in Melrose.

ⓙ you can turn right, on a longer but scenic path back via the Chain Bridge, signed Melrose by River Tweed.

Otherwise, keep ahead to the Dean Road junction and go left, joining the Borders Abbeys Way and immediately branching right through stables on Prior's Walk, which takes a straight line back to Melrose above a mill lade. At a kissing-gate leave Newstead behind then after another keep ahead into Melrose on a residential road. Branch right where it starts to rise, cross the lade and a play park to walk past Melrose Abbey. The path ends opposite the car park. ●

Leaderfoot Viaduct

Constructed of brick and red sandstone, this impressive viaduct spans the River Tweed. It has 19 arches and stands 126 feet (38m) above the water. It was built to carry the Berwickshire Railway and opened in 1865, but was closed in 1948 after floods severed the line elsewhere.

Further Information

Safety on the Hills

The hills, mountains and moorlands of Britain, though of modest height compared with those in many other countries, need to be treated with respect. Friendly and inviting in good weather, they can quickly be transformed into wet, misty, windswept and potentially dangerous areas of wilderness in bad weather. Even on an outwardly fine and settled summer day, conditions can rapidly deteriorate at high altitudes and, in winter, even more so.

Therefore it is advisable always to take both warm and waterproof clothing, sufficient nourishing food, a hot drink, first-aid kit, torch and whistle. Wear suitable footwear, such as strong walking boots or shoes that give a good grip over rocky terrain and on slippery slopes. Try to obtain a local weather forecast and bear it in mind before you start. Do not be afraid to abandon your proposed route and return to your starting point in the event of a sudden and unexpected deterioration in the weather. Do not go alone and allow enough time to finish the walk well before nightfall.

Most of the walks described in this book do not venture into remote wilderness areas and will be safe to do, given due care and respect, at any time of year in all but the most unreasonable weather. Indeed, a crisp, fine winter day often provides perfect walking conditions, with firm ground underfoot and a clarity that is not possible to achieve in the other seasons of the year. A few walks, however, are suitable only for reasonably fit and experienced hill walkers able to use a compass and should definitely not be tackled by anyone else during the winter months or in bad weather, especially high winds and mist. These are indicated in the general description that precedes each of the walks.

Walkers and the Law

Walkers in Scotland have long enjoyed a moral and de facto right of access, now enshrined in *The Land Reform (Scotland) Act 2003*. This carries with it responsibilities, which are outlined in the

Arnton Fell (Walk 13)

Scottish Outdoor Access Code. The three key principles are:

- Respect the interests of other people
- Care for the Environment
- Take responsibility for your own actions

The following common situations affect walkers.
- Farm steadings - There is no legal right of access to farm steadings but in practice many existing routes go through them.
- Fields - Keep to paths where possible or walk around the margins of a field under crops.
- Fences, dykes and hedges - When crossing walls, dykes, fences and hedges use a gate or a stile where possible, otherwise climb over carefully to avoid damage.
- Golf Courses - You have a right of access to cross golf courses but must avoid damage to the playing surface and never step on to the greens. Cross as quickly as possible, considering the rights of the players.
- Deer Stalking - During the hunting season check to ensure that the walks you are planning avoid stalking operations.

More detailed information can be obtained at outdooraccess-scotland.com.

Useful Organisations

Association for the Protection of Rural Scotland
Dolphin House, 4 Hunter Square,
Edinburgh, EH1 1QW
Tel. 0131 225 7012
aprs.scot

Camping and Caravanning Club
Greenfields House, Westwood Way,
Coventry, CV4 8JH
Tel. 024 7647 5426
campingandcaravanningclub.co.uk

Forestry and Land Scotland
Great Glen House, Leachkin Road,
Inverness, IV3 8NW
Tel. 0300 067 6000
forestryandland.gov.scot

Historic Environment Scotland
Longmore House,
Salisbury Place,
Edinburgh, EH9 1SH
Tel. 0131 668 8600
historicenvironment.scot

Hostelling Scotland
7 Glebe Crescent,
Stirling, FK8 2JA
Tel. 0345 293 7373
hostellingscotland.org.uk

National Trust for Scotland
Hermiston Quay,
5 Cultins Road,
Edinburgh, EH11 4DF
Tel. 0131 385 7490
nts.org.uk

NatureScot
Southern Scotland, Galashiels Office
Anderson's Chambers,
Market Place,
Galashiels, TD1 3AF
Tel. 01738 457070
nature.scot

Ordnance Survey
ordnancesurvey.co.uk

Public Transport
Traveline Scotland
travelinescotland.com

Ramblers Scotland
The Melting Pot,
15 Calton Road,
Edinburgh, EH8 8DL
Tel. 0131 357 5850
ramblers.org.uk/scotland

Scottish Rights of Way and Access Society
24 Annandale Street,
Edinburgh, EH7 4AN
Tel. 0131 558 1222
scotways.com

Visitor information
VisitScotland Head Office
Ocean Point One,
94 Ocean Drive, Leith,
Edinburgh, EH6 6JH

Scottish Borders Office
Shepherds Mill, Whinfield Road,
Selkirk, TD7 5DT
Tel. 0131 472 2222
visitscotland.com

iCentre
Jedburgh: 01835 863170

Weather forecast
www.metoffice.gov.uk/weather

Ordnance Survey maps for Scottish Borders

The area is covered by Ordnance Survey 1:50 000 scale (1¼ inches to 1 mile or 2cm to 1km) Landranger sheets 67, 73, 74, 75, 79, and 80. These all-purpose maps are packed with information to help you explore the area. Viewpoints, picnic sites, places of interest, caravan and camping sites are shown, as well as public rights of way information such as footpaths and bridleways.

To examine this area in more detail, and especially if you are planning walks, Ordnance Survey Explorer maps at 1:25 000 (2½ inches to 1 mile or 4cm to 1km) scale are ideal:

OL16   (The Cheviot Hills)
OL42   (Kielder Water & Forest)
330   (Moffat & St Mary's Loch)
331   (Teviotdale South)
337   (Peebles & Innerleithen)
338   (Galashiels, Selkirk & Melrose)
339   (Kelso, Coldstream & Lower Tweed Valley)
346   (Berwick-upon-Tweed)

Ordnance Survey maps and guides are available from most booksellers, stationers and newsagents.

Signpost for multiple routes (Walk 22)

Text:	Felicity Martin; Dennis and Jan Kelsall for Walks 8, 12, 13, 14, 16, 18, 19, 23, 24 and 26 taken from PF (35) Northumberland and Scottish Borders, which has now been superseded
Photography:	Felicity Martin; Dennis and Jan Kelsall
Editorial:	Ark Creative (UK) Ltd
Design:	Ark Creative (UK) Ltd

© Crown copyright / Ordnance Survey Limited, 2023
Published by Milestone Publishing Ltd under licence from Ordnance Survey Limited.
Pathfinder, Ordnance Survey, OS and the OS logos are registered trademarks of
Ordnance Survey Limited and are used under licence from Ordnance Survey Limited.
Text © Milestone Publishing Limited, 2023

This product includes mapping data licensed from Ordnance Survey
© Crown copyright and database rights (2023) OS 150002047

ISBN: 978-0-31909-258-3

While every care has been taken to ensure the accuracy of the route directions, the publishers cannot accept responsibility for errors or omissions, or for changes in details given. The countryside is not static: hedges and fences can be removed, stiles can be replaced by gates, field boundaries can alter, footpaths can be rerouted and changes in ownership can result in the closure or diversion of some concessionary paths. Also, paths that are easy and pleasant for walking in fine conditions may become slippery, muddy and difficult in wet weather, while stepping stones across rivers and streams may become impassable.

If you find an inaccuracy in either the text or maps, please contact Milestone Publishing at the address below.

First published 2023 by Milestone Publishing.

Milestone Publishing, 19-21D Charles Street, Bath, BA1 1HX
pathfinderwalks.co.uk

Printed in India by Replika Press Pvt. Ltd. 1/23

All rights reserved. No part of this publication may be reproduced, transmitted in any form or by any means, or stored in a retrieval system without either the prior written permission of the publisher, or in the case of reprographic reproduction a licence issued in accordance with the terms and licences issued by the CLA Ltd.

A catalogue record for this book is available from the British Library.

Front cover: Eildon Hills from Mertoun Bridge (Walk 11)
Page 1: On the descent from Eildon Hill North (Walk 14)

Pathfinder Guides
Britain's best-loved walking guides

Scotland
Pathfinder Walks
- 3 ISLE OF SKYE
- 4 CAIRNGORMS
- 7 FORT WILLIAM & GLEN COE
- 19 DUMFRIES & GALLOWAY
- 23 LOCH LOMOND, THE TROSSACHS, & STIRLING
- 27 PERTHSHIRE, ANGUS & FIFE
- 30 LOCH NESS & INVERNESS
- 31 OBAN, MULL & KINTYRE
- 46 ABERDEEN & ROYAL DEESIDE
- 47 EDINBURGH, PENTLANDS & LOTHIANS
- 82 ORKNEY & SHETLAND
- 83 NORTH COAST 500 & NORTHERN HIGHLANDS
- 85 OUTER HEBRIDES
- 88 SCOTTISH BORDERS

North of England
Pathfinder Walks
- 15 YORKSHIRE DALES
- 22 MORE LAKE DISTRICT
- 28 NORTH YORK MOORS
- 39 DURHAM, NORTH PENNINES & TYNE AND WEAR
- 42 CHESHIRE
- 49 VALE OF YORK & YORKSHIRE WOLDS
- 53 LANCASHIRE
- 60 LAKE DISTRICT
- 63 PEAK DISTRICT
- 64 SOUTH PENNINES
- 71 THE HIGH FELLS OF LAKELAND
- 73 MORE PEAK DISTRICT
- 86 LAKE DISTRICT & CUMBRIA ACCESSIBLE WALKS
- 87 NORTHUMBERLAND

Short Walks
- 2 PEAK DISTRICT
- 13 NORTH YORK MOORS

Wales
Pathfinder Walks
- 10 SNOWDONIA
- 18 BRECON BEACONS
- 34 PEMBROKESHIRE & CARMARTHENSHIRE
- 41 MID WALES
- 55 GOWER, SWANSEA & CARDIFF
- 78 ANGLESEY, LLEYN & SNOWDONIA
- 79 DEE VALLEY, CLWYDIAN HILLS & NORTH EAST WALES

Short Walks
- 14 SNOWDONIA
- 31 BRECON BEACONS

Heart of England
Pathfinder Walks
- 6 COTSWOLDS
- 20 SHERWOOD FOREST & THE EAST MIDLANDS
- 29 WYE VALLEY & FOREST OF DEAN
- 74 THE MALVERNS TO WARWICKSHIRE
- 80 SHROPSHIRE
- 81 STAFFORDSHIRE
- 84 BERKSHIRE, BUCKINGHAMSHIRE & OXFORDSHIRE

Short Walks
- 4 COTSWOLDS
- 32 HEREFORDSHIRE & THE WYE VALLEY

East of England
Pathfinder Walks
- 44 ESSEX
- 45 NORFOLK
- 48 SUFFOLK
- 50 LINCOLNSHIRE & THE WOLDS
- 51 CAMBRIDGESHIRE & THE FENS

South West of England
Pathfinder Walks
- 1 SOUTH DEVON & DARTMOOR
- 5 CORNWALL
- 9 EXMOOR & THE QUANTOCKS
- 11 DORSET & THE JURASSIC COAST
- 26 DARTMOOR
- 68 NORTH & MID DEVON
- 69 SOUTH WEST ENGLAND'S COAST
- 76 SOMERSET & THE MENDIPS
- 77 WILTSHIRE

Short Walks
- 8 DARTMOOR
- 9 CORNWALL
- 21 EXMOOR
- 29 SOUTH DEVON

South East of England
Pathfinder Walks
- 8 KENT
- 12 NEW FOREST, HAMPSHIRE & SOUTH DOWNS
- 25 THAMES VALLEY & CHILTERNS
- 54 HERTFORDSHIRE & BEDFORDSHIRE
- 65 SURREY
- 66 SOUTH DOWNS NATIONAL PARK & WEST SUSSEX
- 67 SOUTH DOWNS NATIONAL PARK & EAST SUSSEX
- 72 THE HOME COUNTIES FROM LONDON BY TRAIN

Short Walks
- 23 NEW FOREST NATIONAL PARK
- 27 ISLE OF WIGHT

Practical Guide
- 75 NAVIGATION SKILLS FOR WALKERS

City Walks
- LONDON
- OXFORD
- EDINBURGH